CAMBRIDGE LIBRARY COLLECTION

Books of enduring scholarly value

Art and Architecture

From the middle of the eighteenth century, with the growth of travel at home and abroad and the increase in leisure for the wealthier classes, the arts became the subject of more widespread appreciation and discussion. The rapid expansion of book and periodical publishing in this area both reflected and encouraged interest in art and art history among the wider reading public. This series throws light on the development of visual culture and aesthetics. It covers topics from the Grand Tour to the great exhibitions of the nineteenth century, and includes art criticism and biography.

Architectural Notes on German Churches

A tutor of mathematics at Cambridge, William Whewell (1794–1866) mostly published on mechanics. He became professor of mineralogy in 1828, Knightbridge professor of moral philosophy in 1838, and master of Trinity College in 1841. This work is unusual among his writings for its focus on architecture, yet the emphasis placed on terminology is consistent with his other publications, such as *An Essay on Mineralogical Classification and Nomenclature* (1828). *Architectural Notes* is significant for offering a detailed theoretical analysis of the origins of Gothic architecture, especially of the mechanical principles underlying it, notably the pointed arch. The discussion of German churches, despite the book's title, is of secondary concern, although guidance is given for recording Gothic buildings. This first edition was published anonymously in 1830. The second (1835) and third (1842) editions bore Whewell's name and were partially revised to reflect recent research on the origin of the pointed arch.

Cambridge University Press has long been a pioneer in the reissuing of out-of-print titles from its own backlist, producing digital reprints of books that are still sought after by scholars and students but could not be reprinted economically using traditional technology. The Cambridge Library Collection extends this activity to a wider range of books which are still of importance to researchers and professionals, either for the source material they contain, or as landmarks in the history of their academic discipline.

Drawing from the world-renowned collections in the Cambridge University Library and other partner libraries, and guided by the advice of experts in each subject area, Cambridge University Press is using state-of-the-art scanning machines in its own Printing House to capture the content of each book selected for inclusion. The files are processed to give a consistently clear, crisp image, and the books finished to the high quality standard for which the Press is recognised around the world. The latest print-on-demand technology ensures that the books will remain available indefinitely, and that orders for single or multiple copies can quickly be supplied.

The Cambridge Library Collection brings back to life books of enduring scholarly value (including out-of-copyright works originally issued by other publishers) across a wide range of disciplines in the humanities and social sciences and in science and technology.

Architectural Notes
on German Churches

With Remarks on the Origin
of Gothic Architecture

WILLIAM WHEWELL

CAMBRIDGE
UNIVERSITY PRESS

CAMBRIDGE UNIVERSITY PRESS

Cambridge, New York, Melbourne, Madrid, Cape Town,
Singapore, São Paolo, Delhi, Mexico City

Published in the United States of America by Cambridge University Press, New York

www.cambridge.org
Information on this title: www.cambridge.org/9781108051767

© in this compilation Cambridge University Press 2013

This edition first published 1830
This digitally printed version 2013

ISBN 978-1-108-05176-7 Paperback

Plate III.

J. & E. S. Storer, so Cambridge.

Laach. from the N.W.

ARCHITECTURAL NOTES

ON

GERMAN CHURCHES,

WITH

REMARKS

ON THE

Origin of Gothic Architecture.

CAMBRIDGE:

Printed by J. Smith, Printer to the University;

FOR J. & J. J. DEIGHTON, CAMBRIDGE;

AND SOLD BY

LONGMAN, REES, ORME, BROWN & GREEN, LONDON.

M.D.CCC.XXX.

CONTENTS.

CHAP. II.

OF THE CHARACTERS OF TRANSITION OR EARLY GERMAN ARCHITECTURE.

CHAP. III.

SUGGESTIONS ON THE METHOD OF MAKING ARCHITECTURAL NOTES.

DESCRIPTION OF THE PLATES.

PLATE I. Represents the steps which form the transition from circular to pointed vaulting. Fig. 1. is Roman vaulting (see p. 6.), the vault-arches in both directions being semi-circular. Fig. 2. represents the kind of vaulting called Welch vaulting, which was necessary when the length and breadth of the vaulted space were different, and both were covered with semi-circular vaults. Fig. 3. shews the way in which this form was avoided (p. 7; and p. 23, No. 6.) the vault-arch in one direction being still semi-circular, and this vault being crossed by another pointed one, of the same height but smaller width. Fig. 4. (p. 7; and p. 23, No. 6.) has pointed vault-arches both ways. Fig. 5. (p. 25, No. 8.) represents sex-partite vaulting; all the vaults being pointed. Fig. 7. is octopartite vaulting on a square base, and Fig. 8. octopartite vaulting on an octagonal base (p. 26. and 27. Nos 9. and 10.). For Fig. 6. see Plate 4.

Under the figures in this plate are placed the symbols which would represent the vaulting according to the system explained page 75.

PLATE II. Three Ground Plans with their vaulting, (see p. 37). Fig. 9, the Cathedral at Mentz, represents a Roman-esque Cathedral, with both east and west apses, two tran-septs, towers at each crossing, and a pair of towers at each end (p. 39). The vaulting of the east apse is a semi-dome (p. 13.), of the west apse, polygonal with acute cells (p. 27). The vaulting of the center aisle is groined, with only the transverse ribs pointed (p. 24); the next lateral aisles are Roman vault-ing; the exterior aisles are of more modern work, and are pointed both ways.

Fig. 10, St. Aposteln at Cologne. A transverse-triapsal church, with a large western tower; two smaller towers at the east, and an octagonal pyramid at the eastern crossing. (See p. 39). It has also a western transept. The apses are vaulted with semi-domes : the old vaulting of the center aisle is sex-partite on the double compartments, and cylindrical on the single ones; the modern vaulting (represented by dotted lines) has acute transverse vaults over each single compartment, the longitudinal vault being semi-circular. (See p. 26, 54, and 76).

Fig. 11, Abbey Church of Laach. A parallel-triapsal church, (see p. 54.), with a semi-circular apse at each end, a pair of square towers at the east, and of round towers at the west, two transepts and towers at the two crossings. (See p. 39). The three aisles have each Roman vaulting in single compartments. There are three apses towards the east, each with a semi-dome. A portal-cloister, (see p. 61.) occurs at the west end.

These Plans were drawn by the eye without any measurement, and have no pretensions to exactness of proportions or details.

PLATE III. Perspective view of Laach, exhibiting the six towers just mentioned, with their galleries, windows, pan-nelling, corbel-tables, gables and roofing. (See p. 39). The semi-circular *west* end also is shewn, and part of the portal-cloister.

PLATE IV. Fig. 6. Part of a Romanesque Cathedral, with Roman vaulting in double compartments ; shewing the origin of the triforium-space, clerestory, alternate piers, and clerestory windows in pairs. (See p. 19).

Fig. 12. A compartment of the church at Sinzig, drawn in memorandum lines only, (see p. 78.), exhibiting the principal and intermediate piers, vaulting pillars, triforium, and fan-shaped clerestory windows. (See p. 51).

Fig. 13. Ground Plan of a pier of engaged shafts and pier edges. (See p. 45).

Fig. 14. Ground Plan of pillar, with square abacuses set obliquely. (See p. 52).

Fig. 15. Cornice which occurs over the apsidal gallery. (See p. 58).

PREFACE.

THE following pages contain the substance of some notes on churches, made during a rapid tour through a part of Germany, with a few remarks suggested by what I there observed. The matter contained in them appears to me to add something to our published information on this subject; and I am persuaded, that by extending and arranging similar observations, we should be led to some interesting and satisfactory views on the progress of ecclesiastical architecture in Germany.

As I see no prospect of my having leisure to pursue the point myself, I place these materials in the hands of the public; with the hope that they may stimulate or assist others, who may take up the subject with better opportunities of doing it justice.

It might perhaps be worth while to publish these memoranda, even if I had no other object than to guide and assist, in some measure, those who may visit Germany with a wish to study

a

the ecclesiastical architecture of the country. I have myself felt how welcome to a traveller so employed, are the smallest and most imperfect hints of what he is to see. A single phrase, especially from any one whose studies have been architectural, may direct him to objects which will give him the greatest pleasure, or may save him from a tedious journey, ending in the unprofitable magnificence of some Italianizing church. It will, I think, appear from the following pages, that there are abundant sources of interest to the English antiquary in the country through which I travelled, and that the German churches, both from their resemblances and from their differences as compared with our own, may eminently illustrate the subject of church architecture, which has so long been in our country a favorite topic of speculation.

I cannot, however, pretend to deny, that I have mixed up with these indications and statements something of theory and system. This has taken place almost without my having intended it. It so happened, that the churches which came under my notice in the neighbourhood of the Rhine, illustrated very remarkably an opinion which had long appeared to me almost certain, with regard to the introduction of the pointed arch. Some of the modes of building assumed in this theory, which had been only hypothetical suppositions when it was applied to

English churches, were found existing as common architectural practices in Germany. It seemed worth while to explain to others this curious coincidence of the theoretical and actual progress of things: and I was thus led to arrange my observations on German churches in subordination to this view. The consequence has been, that this Essay has partly assumed the shape of a disquisition on the origin of Gothic Architecture, instead of that of a collection of architectural notes, which was the form originally contemplated.

The doctrine which seems to me so probable is, as may be seen in the following pages, that the adoption of the pointed arch in vaulted roofs arose from the requirements of vaulting, and from the necessity of having arches of equal heights with different widths: and it appears moreover that the succession of contrivances to which these circumstances gave birth, is found more completely developed, and probably more ancient, in the German edifices than in our own.

If it be allowed that this account of the origin of the pointed arch is the true one, it will perhaps be granted without much difficulty that, from its original situation in the vaulting, this form of arch was gradually diffused into every other part of the building. This opinion accordingly I am disposed to entertain, though I do not consider it to be susceptible of the same exactness of proof as the former tenet: and I have tried to shew that this was the manner in which the old system of architecture, derived from the classical styles, was finally converted into one of a different and opposite kind. According to this view all the other changes which are found in company with the newly-adopted pointed arch, may be considered as the natural manifestations of the new character thus impressed upon art. The features and details of the later architecture were brought out more and more completely, in proportion as the *idea*, or internal principle of unity and harmony in the newer works, became clear and single, like that which had pervaded the buildings of antiquity: the characteristic forms of the one being horizontal, reposing, definite; of the other vertical, aspiring, indefinite*.

---

* The contrast of character which exists between the Grecian and the Gothic styles is well marked by Mr. Rickman. But the various rules and arrangements which he has pointed out as opposite in the two systems, combine in each case to make a common impression on the mind, and flow from some fundamental principle. It is suggested to me by a friend, that this distinctive principle of construction in the Gothic architecture appears to be the admission of oblique pressures, and inclined lines of support. In Grecian architecture the whole edifice consists of horizontal masses reposing on vertical props. In Gothic buildings on the contrary, the pointed arch is always to be considered as formed by two sides leaning against each other at top, and pressing outward at their lower ends. The eye recognizes this statical condition in the leading lines of the edifice, and requires the details to
conform

It does not appear that the degree of attention which the circumstance so well deserves, has
yet been given to the extraordinary uniformity
of one particular style of Gothic architecture, as
it is found over a large part of Europe. The
style to which I refer, belongs to that which
Mr. Rickman has called "The Decorated*," in

---

conform to it. We have thus in the Grecian buildings nothing
but rectangular forms and spaces: horizontal lines with vertical ones subordinate to them. The pediment is one mass
with its horizontal cornice, and does not violate this rule.
Arches, when they occur, are either subordinate parts, or
mark the transition style, in which the integrity of the principle is no longer preserved. In Gothic works, on the other
hand, the arch is an indispensable and governing feature: it
has pillars to support its vertical, and buttresses to resist its
lateral pressure: its summit may be carried upwards indefinitely by the joint thrust of its two sides. All the parts
agree in this character of indefinite upward extension, with
an inclination or flexure to allow of their meeting at top ; and
thus obviously require and depend on pressures acting obliquely.

* Mr. Rickman's terms " Early English," " Decorated,"
" Perpendicular" architecture, have been objected to. It is
a sufficient reason for continuing to employ these words, that
they have been so much more accurately defined and discri-
minated than any other terms of classification. But I conceive
that some of the objections which have been raised against these
names, have arisen from not attending precisely to the views
with which they were imposed. They were apparently intended to distinguish each style from the *preceding* one: and
for this purpose they are significant enough. The *Decorated*
differs principally from the Early English in exhibiting a
greater degree of decoration: the *Perpendicular* varies from
the later Decorated mainly in having certain perpendicular
members,

its earlier form, and with a prevalence of circular tracery. The cathedral of Cologne may be
taken as the great type or exemplar of this style;
it corresponds pretty nearly in character with
such English buildings as the east end of Lincoln cathedral, the chapter-house and nave of
York, the nave of Exeter. St. Ouen at Rouen,
the choir at Amiens, are French examples. Germany and the Low Countries abound with them:
along with Cologne we may mention Altenburg, Oppenheim, Strasburg. This mode of
architecture seems, in fact, to have occupied
almost the whole of Europe, at least north of
the Alps, with a singular identity of spirit and
character; and with a very remarkable uniformity
in subordinate members, and even in minute
details. In different countries it succeeded, apparently in different manners, the previous architecture which had been formed by an imperfect
imitation of Roman models: and in each case,
when the architects have entirely emancipated
themselves from the forms of this degraded Ro-

---

members, mullions, which in the Decorated are not perpendicular throughout. And the term *Rectilinear*, which has
been suggested, would not apparently be an advantageous sub-
stitute for Perpendicular ; for the mullions, the only members
to which the description applies distinctively, are rectilinear
only so far as they are perpendicular. The term " Early
English " has *accidentally* a peculiar propriety, inasmuch as
this style is found almost exclusively in England: at least it
does not occur in Germany.

man, they fall into the same new style; which
thus seems to afford, in each country, a goal
and resting place after a period of progression
and change.

In England, indeed, the case was somewhat peculiar. We possess a style, the "Early
English" of Mr. Rickman, preceding that Decorated to which we have ascribed this European
diffusion; and this style may be considered as
retaining very few traces of the Roman or
Romanesque character. It may be said that
with us the Gothic system was fully established
when this style had become universal*. Though
fully established, however, the new character was
not thus completely matured. The differences
between this English architecture and the Complete Gothic of the Continent are clearly marked;
and it is obvious that the additional changes introduced in the latter are such as to present a still
further developement of the Gothic principles.
The abundant use of window-tracery in the latter
case, compared with its entire absence in the former, is a sufficiently broad distinction; and besides this difference, the modes of clustering the
shafts and mouldings, and of forming the but-

---

* What is here said will shew in what sense I have in the
following pages used the phrase "Complete Gothic." In Germany it designates the Decorated style, because there they
have no previous fully developed Gothic: but in England it
includes both the Early English and the Decorated.

tresses and windows, are limited with a sort of
severity and monotony in the Early English style,
which, in the continental edifices of this, and the
English edifices of the next period, is exchanged
for a freer, more flexible, and more fertile rule.

It seems to me a most curious fact, that the
English architects should have gone by a path
of their own to the consummation of Gothic
architecture, and should on the road have discovered a style, full of beauty and unity, and
quite finished in itself, which escaped their German brother-artists. It will, I think, be proved
that this is the case, by any one who examines
the German churches. Those of them which belong to the steps of the transition from the Roman manner to that of Cologne, have nowhere
a character clear and independent, and distinct
from either of those. They differ by gradations
of more or less, by changes of one part or another, the style advancing over the interval without apparently finding any intermediate position
of equilibrium. For the sake of collecting into
one view the phenomena of this transition, and
of noting local peculiarities, I have given an enumeration of the characters of *Early German* architecture. But by this term I designate, not a
single and definite style like the *Early English*
of Salisbury and Lincoln, but the collection of
all the forms which occur after the great change
had begun, and before it was completed; from

the just-wavering Romanesque of Mentz or
Worms, to the multiplied but not quite Gothic
elements of Limburg and Gelnhausen.

I fear that some of my readers may expect
to find in the following pages more information
than I have given, concerning the dates of particular buildings, or the exact chronology of the
different styles of architecture. I am obliged to
abstain, at present, from entering directly upon
this field. I am well aware that such discussions might be more interesting than description
and theory can hope to be; and it is undeniable
that those enquiries are very essential to complete our knowledge of architectural history.
But strong reasons withhold my pen from such
topics. The unavoidable length to which these
antiquarian lucubrations spread, and the quantity
of time and learning which they require, may
excuse their absence from a small and subsi-
diary essay like the present one: and besides this
consideration, there seems to be an advantage in
studying separately the two things which we are
afterwards to compare; — the differences of style,
and the differences of date. If there really be
any consistency and uniformity in the several
buildings of the same epoch, we ought to be
able to detect this agreement by examining the
buildings alone: and when we are satisfied of
this common character, we shall know what
problem we have to solve in investigating *when*

and *how* these epochs followed each other. We
have to compare the *internal* evidence of deri-
vation or succession with the *external* evidence
of time; and what I have here contributed, is
intended to illustrate the former term of this
comparison.

To tell the truth, the difficulties of the historical branch of the enquiry are sufficient to deter
any one from engaging himself hastily in its per-
plexities. The paucity and indistinctness of the
notices of the erection of early buildings; the
difficulty of identifying those described with those
that still exist; the confusion of works protracted,
suspended, built in imitation of others, or in accommodation to them; the alternation of destruc-
tions and reparations; —all the chances that can
happen to edifices or to authors, combine to un-
settle the faith of the architectural antiquary.
And the lesson thus taught us seems to be, that
though we are to examine the history of particular
buildings as carefully as we possibly can, we
are not to give to any one of them too great
a weight in determining our architectural chronology; but to take rather the age which is col-
lectively inferred from many resembling churches.

If we reject this maxim, we may be left in
no small embarrassment; and this, in fact, seems
to have befallen the architectural enquirers of
modern times; as, for instance, in the case of
Coutances. The cathedral of Coutances in Nor-

mandy is, for the most part, in a style which
has a great resemblance to our Early English,
and appears to be not less advanced than our
good buildings of that class.   Its towers have
tall pointed windows, divided into two lights by
single or double slender shafts; they have clustered shafts at their corners, and octagonal
turrets, also decorated with shafts, and finished
with a pyramid of stone.   The interior in like
manner has throughout pointed arches, abund-
ance of small roll mouldings, slender shafts with
capitals of upright leaves, variously clustered,
grouped, and supported by corbels; the profiles
of piers and of mouldings, the vaulting, the triforium balustrade, the clerestory windows, are all
in the same style.   In short the cathedral is
decidedly Early Gothic, with few or no traces
of Romanesque or Norman.   This Early Gothic,
or, as we term it, Early English style, is by
the best authorities held to have made its appearance among us about 1189; and it has been
commonly believed, that the generality of churches
in France agree pretty well with this English
epoch.   But if we receive the date which the
best evidence seems to fix for Coutances, we shall
have the new style fully developed in Normandy
a century and a half too early for this doctrine.
M. Gerville, in the first volume of the Memoirs
of the Academy of Antiquaries of Normandy,
has endeavoured to shew that the church in ques-

tion was built and dedicated before the year 1056; and he has offered evidence better than can generally be had in such cases, to prove that the building, of which the Monkish chronicler gives us this account, was not replaced by another at a time more consistent with the received theory. This case is important, because the anomaly at Coutances is not the pointed arch only, which may probably be produced of as early a date in other instances, but the whole style of the building, which according to M. Gerville's view is an anticipation by 130 years, of our architecture.

There appears to be a case in Germany almost as rebellious as Coutances to established opinions, in the cathedral of Bamberg. This church is an instance of what I have called Early German architecture. It has pointed pier arches, and pointed vaulting; the piers have slender shafts attached, the mouldings are small rolls; there are clustered and banded shafts with capitals of upright foliage; a polygonal west apse, vaulted with very acute cells, and many similar features. The German antiquaries would agree very nearly with our English ones, in attributing this building, from the evidence of its style, to a period somewhere about the middle of the 12th century. But it seems, that so far as the external evidence goes, we must take a date considerably earlier. The foundation of the bishopric of Bamberg by the emperor Henry II. in 1007, is an event which occupies a prominent place in German history; and in connection with this occurrence, we find that the cathedral which had been already begun, was dedicated in 1012. Bishop Otto, who held the See from 1104 to 1130, is stated to have rebuilt the west end, which had suffered by a fire; and accordingly there are in this part the features of a style somewhat later than that of the eastern choir.

In the same manner the church of St. George at Limburg on the Lahn, which shews a still more clear approximation to the Gothic, is said to have been finished in 1058. It is exceedingly difficult to reconcile such statements with the character of buildings which are known to belong to dates approaching these.

The succession of the earlier style seems to be preserved unbroken in existing edifices. Spires, Mentz and Worms, are spoken of in the succeeding pages as three great examples of the Romanesque; and the greater part of these mighty edifices is clearly and altogether different from the succeeding style. Of these buildings the dates are said to be historically known. Spires was founded by Conrad II. in 1030, and finished in 1061. The east end of Worms is earlier still, and is of the time of Henry II. (who died 1024.). The oldest part of Mentz is said to be of the date of Archbishop Willigis, between 978 and 1009.

These buildings, except Spires, have pointed arches in the vaulting, but all the other arches and openings are round, and the members altogether Romanesque. Other remains in Germany enable us· to pursue still further back the Romanesque architecture. St. Mary Capitoline at Cologne is said to be incontestably of the ninth century: the chapel at Lorch, so eminently Roman in its character, is attributed to the same age; and if we include Italian buildings in our researches, there will probably be no difficulty in tracing the gradations of this architecture from the classical times, to the period when the rudiments of the newer style begin to prevail.

But if we descend in the order of time, it seems to be a much harder task to determine the epoch and progress of the transition from the Romanesque to the Gothic. It does not appear that the dates of the transition churches of Germany are generally known there; even buildings of considerable splendor belonging to this class, as Gelnhausen, Andernach, Boppart, are dated by writers according to internal evidence only: and the cases where we have other testimony, as Bamberg and Limburg, serve rather to make the matter more obscure. We may however hope for much light from the spirit of research and interest on this subject, which appears at present to be so extensively and actively at work in the neighbourhood of many of these edifices.

If we descend still further, we find ourselves among buildings of which the date is somewhat more certain: and the period of the full developement of the Gothic style may perhaps be fixed with some accuracy. And it would appear, that this style in Germany belongs to a time somewhat earlier than the *resembling* style in England, though not so early as the earliest *good Gothic* in this country. The same also appears to be the case in France, so far as the investigations of Dr. Whittington and others have gone. If we take the dates of the most conspicuous examples of Early Gothic buildings, we find them as follows. The *Early English* of Salisbury and of the south transept of York belongs to about 1220. Westminster, also of good Early English work, was begun in 1245, by Henry III. The *Decorated* Architecture of Germany treads close on the heels of this. Cologne was begun in 1248: the front of Strasburg built in 1276. The resembling examples in our own country are but a little later. The presbytery of Lincoln is of 1282, retaining much of the Early English in its character. The chapter-house of York, and the nave of Exeter come in later, between 1291 and 1330: the chapter-house of Wells between 1293 and 1302. Oppenheim was built between 1262 and 1317, and is of a more advanced character than our English buildings of that date. The window-tracery is of the

flowing kind; the walls are covered with pannelling and feathering; and their remarkably small
thickness (they are not more than 18 inches) is
supported by rich and deep buttresses with
crocketting, &c. The nave of York has flowing
tracery, and is said to be after 1320. Amiens,
which is generally compared with Salisbury, being nearly of the same date, is incontestably
more advanced in style, having window-tracery,
triangular canopies, crockets, pannelling, &c. Indeed it is not difficult to conceive why the English
architects did not adopt, so soon as the Germans
and French, all the Decorated features; for we
may easily imagine that they would abandon with
regret the beautiful simplicity and sobriety of the
Early English, even for the rich and elegant complexity of the succeeding style.

It will be a matter of great interest to obtain hereafter, as it may be hoped we shall, a
more accurate and extensive comparison of the
synchronisms of Gothic architecture in different
parts of Europe. Another curious enquiry which
as yet has not been critically pursued, is, over
what geographical extent of countries the genuine
Gothic style prevailed.

It has no doubt been widely diffused, but probably has not so completely covered the face of
Europe as is often imagined So long indeed as
Gothic was synonymous with *barbarous*, and was
applied to all architecture which deviated from the

classical rule and spirit, it was easy to find Gothic in every European country, and even in other quarters of the globe. But if we use the term Gothic in a definite sense, to designate a kind of architecture which has its principle of unity no less than the classical, and of which those only are genuine features which we find in good examples constructed upon this principle, we shall learn to restrict the local extent of this style within narrower limits. These limits I hope will hereafter be defined by those who give their attention to this branch of art. Going eastward, I know that the style extends as far as Magdeburg in the north, and Vienna in the south of Germany. On the west, it is said that there are in Spain good cathedrals of Gothic architecture. Those at Segovia, Toledo and Burgos are particularly mentioned; and I should think it likely that the last of these three for instance, is of proper Gothic character, though hardly of the pure style of the best time, since it was built by German architects, John of Cologne and his son Simon, after the year 1442. The Moorish architecture of Spain, from which some writers have endeavoured to derive the Gothic, is certainly not Gothic, and is connected with that style only by slight and superficial resemblances.

I am not so much acquainted with Italy as to be able to pronounce whether the true Gothic

found its way over the Alps. So far as one can
judge by barely passing to the Italian side of
that barrier, the tramontane architecture was
never fairly established in the country. The great
cathedrals of the middle ages in the Italian cities,
exhibit a most curious and peculiar Romanesque,
but this did not, as in the more northern regions,
transform itself into a new and independent style.
It is indeed easy to imagine that the spirit of
the classical ages never ceased to haunt the
efforts of Italian art: and that whatever propen-
sities did arise towards a set of forms different
from the antique, were perpetually interrupted in
their developement by the surviving models and
maxims of the ancient times. The tendencies
opposite to the Roman system, instead of being
freely and energetically pursued till the result
was another system, were checked and thwarted as
fast as they appeared; not eradicated indeed, but
blighted in their bud. Before the Italian artists
had fully seized the principles which had been so
well followed out in Germany, these principles
were again overturned by the revival of classical
architecture along with classical literature.

The cathedral of Milan is so celebrated as a
grand Gothic edifice*, that I shall perhaps be

* Madame de Stael, whose words may be taken as an
expression of the popular admiration, says in her Corinne,
that this edifice is the master-piece of Gothic art in Italy, as
St. Peter's is of Roman.

excused, if I speak of this church in particular.
I regret to have to dissent where others admire,
but I am obliged to say, that Milan has no claim
to be considered as a good example of Gothic
architecture. In order to possess excellence in
this, as in any other style, a work must have the
requisite parts clearly exhibited and well-propor-
tioned. Now the principal parts of the interior
of a cathedral are, as is explained in the following
Essay, the piers, the pier-arches, the triforium,
the clerestory, and the vaulting. At Milan,
scarcely one of these members can receive a cri-
tical approbation. The *piers* are of imposing
bulk and height, but lose much of their due
effect from having no proper capitals: and the
group of niches which crowns each pier, dis-
placing the capital, ruins entirely the relation of
these supports to the rest of the edifice. The
pier-arches, thus cut off from their pillars, and
thrown into obscurity, hardly catch the eye. There
is not any attempt at a *triforium*: and the *clerestory* also is quite frittered away by being cut
into two portions on each side. For there are five
aisles, and of these the center one is higher than
the two immediately adjacent, and these again
than the exterior aisles, the clear elevation of
each higher part being pierced by small windows.
In this way a single clerestory wall of sufficient
elevation is replaced by two smaller descents; and
thus this member loses all its characteristic appear-

b 2

ance.   Lastly, the *vaulting* is not striking as an architectural work, though very brilliant as to its painted decoration.   If we pass from the interior to the exterior, we shall still find a defect of consistent architectural principle.   The west front, though fringed with pinnacles, is not formed of decided Gothic features: the sloping lines of the magnificent flying buttresses, strongly marked and often repeated, become the leading lines of the building, because they are not stopped and controlled by commanding masses of vertical pinnacles at their lower ends, as is the case at Cologne, and other genuine Gothic churches which possess such members.   Finally, even the forest of pinnacles which crowns this gorgeous edifice fails to give an upward character to its outline: for each of these pinnacles is a well-executed statue; and though such ornaments, *in subordination* to other upright masses, are quite consistent with the Gothic spirit, they are felt, in the present instance, to transgress this condition: the numerical strength of this marble army makes it the governing power; the statuary domineers over the architecture; and we collect, out of all this host of personages and attitudes, no definite lines and regular forms, such as alone can give architectural effect.

If the reader will refer to pages 1 and 2, where I have endeavoured to draw the contrast between the characters of Romanesque and of

Gothic architecture, he will see how impossible
it is, consistently with the principles there enun-
ciated, to give the name of genuine Gothic
architecture to that of Milan; although the passage was written with no reference to that particular example, and expressed merely a general
impression collected from a comparison of many
buildings. In Milan, several of "the mouldings,
cornices, and capitals" *have* "classical forms*;" in
various parts, for instance in the front, "rectangular surfaces, pilasters and entablatures" do *not*
disappear; the enrichments are introduced "by
sculpturing surfaces," *rather than* "by repeating

---

* I speak of course of the part which aspires to the character of Gothic architecture, according to the statement in the
inscription on the front itself; not of the doors and windows,
parts of the former front of Italian architecture, which were
spared "on account of the elegance of the workmanship," and
remain encased in the present façade. I insert here the inscription to which I refer.

TEMPLI . FRONTEM

GRÆCO . OPERE . INCHOATAM

GOTHICO

AD . MOLIS . UNIVERSÆ

CONSENSUM

INSTAURANDAM . PERFICIENDAM

OSTIORUM . LUMINUM

ANTEPAGMENTIS

OB . ARTIFICII . ELEGANTIAM

INTACTIS

XX . VIRI . ÆDIFICATIONI

PROCURANDÆ . DECREVERUNT

ANNO . MDCCLXXXX.

and multiplying the component parts," and there is *not* "a predominance of vertical lines and members.

If we would employ the term *barbarous* with any significance, it is not to be applied, I conceive, to one style of art merely because it differs from another. A Gothic building is no more barbarous than a Grecian one, if the ideas which govern its forms be fully understood and executed; but those attempts rather are to be called barbarous which imitate the features of good models, and which, not catching the principle of the art, exhibit such parts incongruously combined and imperfectly developed. In writing Greek, an Anglicism is a barbarism: but we shall not now be willing to allow English to be barbarous because it is not Greek; and a mixture of the two is equally barbarous whether it pretends to be one or the other.

When the questions have been investigated which concern the formation and diffusion of the general European Gothic, there is another enquiry which remains to be pursued in order to complete the history of the art, and which offers interesting comparisons and curious details. In the same manner in which different and distant nations of Europe converged by different paths to a sort of central idea of Gothic, it appears that they afterwards diverged, and formed out of this common style various degenerate kinds of

architecture different in different countries. In
all the cases, the nature of the change was, that
the ornaments became more profuse and universally applied, the small parts more multiplied and
more like one another; the large features and
portions less marked and dominant. Of the deri-
vatives of the Gothic which thus appeared after it
had lost something of its original purity, perhaps
the most beautiful and the least degenerate is
that which we have in England, the Perpendicular or *Tudor* architecture. In some cases indeed, this style possesses so much boldness and
breadth of parts, combined with its fulness and
richness of detail, as to be scarcely inferior to
any form of Gothic architecture. The style of
degraded Gothic which occurs in France, has
been distinguished by the term *Burgundian.*
(See Quarterly Review for April 1821, p. 126.)
It has great community of character, though considerable differences of detail when compared
with our Tudor architecture. It seems to be
marked by a peculiar form of arch, the elliptical
or flat-topped, as the Tudor style is characterized
by the four-centered arch. In the Netherlands
we have another form of the decline of the
Gothic, which we may call the *Belgian* style, in
the magnificent town-houses of Ghent, Louvain,
&c., of which the architecture, though very celebrated, has not, so far as I know, been critically
examined. It appears in like manner, that the

edifices of the period corresponding to this in
Germany have their peculiarities, and these, like
the last, have not, I believe, been selected and
brought together.

All these forms of architecture, and perhaps
others which are requisite to complete the examination, would be interesting subjects of research.   They were the medium through which
the art became advantageously applicable to do-
mestic and civil, as well as to religious and
warlike, purposes.   With these styles, properly
speaking, commence the magnificence of streets
and cities, the beauty and splendour of the houses
of the great.

Whether or not what I have said may produce conviction on speculative points, on subjects
where language is necessarily vague and demon-
stration impossible, I hope that those parts of
the following work which are descriptive, will be
found sufficiently intelligible by those who prefer facts to theories, that is, particular facts to
general ones.   And I trust that the classifications there employed are only such as may give
clearness and connexion to the descriptions.   Descriptions in detail without some classification
are scarcely readable; and it is only by comparison of resemblances and differences that our
observations become either instructive or interesting.   I have therefore attempted to refer buildings to their places in the order of art, instead

of giving from my note book a succession of extracts relating to particular churches. The style which I have more especially endeavoured to characterize, the Transition or Early German, has not yet, so far as I know, received much distinct attention. Dr. Moller, however, in the course of his valuable Denkmaehler, has recently given us excellent representations of the cathedral at Limburg on the Lahn, which is a very admirable specimen of this kind; and has noticed the intermediate and transition place which this edifice seems to occupy in the developement of the German style.

Though, in the second chapter of the ensuing Essay, I have professed to describe only the Transition style, it will be found, I believe, that I have also mentioned most of the characters of the Romanesque, in the way either of contrast or parallel. Of the complete Gothic I have said less, inasmuch as my object is not to give a complete account of church architecture, but to point out what is peculiar to the German churches, and illustrative of the formation of the Gothic style.

In architectural description I have ventured to employ a few new phrases: or rather, I have fixed and limited the meaning of some of the phrases which I have used, with a view to their being employed steadily and precisely for the future. I hope the courteous reader will not

consider this to be a criminal assumption of philo-
logical power. It is scarcely possible to describe
new features without thus much of innovation, or
to describe any thing distinctly without thus much
of technicality.   Mr. Rickman has shewn, that
by the careful use of terms well selected and
previously defined, language may convey almost
as exact and complete an idea of a building as
can be got from the reality or the pencil : but
in order to do this with the greatest advantage,
our architectural vocabulary should be much extended.   We may learn from the descriptive
sciences, as for instance Botany, how much may
be taught by means of a copious and scientific
terminology; and architects are already in pos-
session of a very numerous list of terms of art
which refer to the Classical Orders; so full, indeed, that there could scarcely ever be much
difficulty in describing a building belonging to
that style.   To establish a complete language
for Gothic architecture, is a proceeding which
might not be beyond the jurisdiction of our emi-
nent architectural authorities; but such a language would require to be illustrated by abundant
drawings and references.   I have not pretended
to invent or define any words except such as I
had occasion for in my own descriptions*.

---

* Among the liberties taken with language for which I
ought to apologize, perhaps I should mention the employment
of

Most persons who attend to ecclesiastical architecture are in the habit, more or less, of making memoranda of noticeable churches which they see. It seems likely that this task might be executed more completely and expeditiously, by following a fixed plan in the selection and arrangement of the parts described. I should even conceive that when a person has to make notes upon several churches, it might be advantageous to prepare a regular skeleton-form or tabular schedule, in which the same blanks should be filled up according to the peculiarities of each instance; and the register thus formed of the members of our churches, would probably be more secure from omission and more easy of comparison, than accounts drawn up at random: at any rate this mode of proceeding, though it might be thought needlessly formal, would make the persons who agreed together to use it, more intelligible to one another. I have

---

of the word *aisle* for the central space (nave or choir,) as well as for the lateral spaces, of a building separated by longitudinal rows of pillars. I believe I am far from being the introducer of this phraseology; and though etymology is, I fear, against me in the use of this word, I can find no other which applies to the three spaces of which it was necessary for me to speak in common.

I have added at the end of this Preface, a note on the mode of describing certain forms of vaulting which are very common in England, but which I had not occasion to refer to in speaking of foreign churches.

not ventured to construct such a skeleton church; but I have recommended what appears to me to be the best order to follow in dissecting any proposed example, as may be seen in Chap. III.

In taking notes of vaulting, I found that the form of the construction could often be expressed both more briefly and more clearly by means of a few lines of rude drawing, than by words; and the marks which I thus employed gradually assumed the character of systematic symbols. Since these are few and simple, and, as it appears to me, easily understood, I have given them with their explanation for the benefit of any architect who may be willing to make a trial of such aid. Besides these marks, which can hardly be called drawing, no skill in drawing is absolutely necessary for the architectural observer, though such skill may of course be very valuable when it exists. Some of the most desirable drawings may be made sufficiently well without the draftsman's eye and hand; for example, profiles of mouldings, which are very important elements, and should be copied; since those of Gothic work cannot be exactly conveyed by means of any terms which have yet obtained reception among architects.

In spite of all that I have said in commendation of verbal descriptions in architecture, I am well aware that most of my readers would prefer receiving information from drawings of buildings; and for their sakes I regret that my plates are so few and so humble. There exist, however, several valuable works with good plates on the subject of German architecture, and more will probably appear in a short time. Dr. Moller's work (Denkmaehler der Deutschen Baukunst) already contains excellent specimens of every style of German buildings, and offers additional interest and beauty in each new number: Mr. Müller's work on Oppenheim, mentioned in the following pages, is of almost unequalled splendour of execution: Dr. Boisserée's magnificent engravings of the Cathedral at Cologne are already known and admired in this country. Besides these, a work on the architecture of the Upper Rhine is publishing at Freyburg in the Brisgau; and I believe some others have appeared which I have not seen. With the spirit which now prevails among Germans on such subjects, we may expect them still further to add to this stock of such representations, as they certainly have still abundant materials for their labours. If Dr. Boisserée, after the completion of his work on the Cathedral of Cologne, should execute his design of giving to the world the other churches of that city and neighbourhood, it will be an invaluable contribution to these studies. Other works, which we may perhaps hope to see, are —an adequate description of the very curious and ancient abbey church at Laach:—a comparative

account of the three great Romanesque cathedrals of Mentz, Spires and Worms, a work
which would have a singular interest:—a worthy
description of the very beautiful cathedral of
Bamberg:—and representations of the many admirable and important specimens of architecture
which are to be found in the city and neighbourhood of Nuremberg.   Such works as these
will enable men to speculate with profit and
pleasure on the history and character of German
architecture.   And when we consider the great
learning and diligent observation of the German antiquarians; their pleasure in the beauties
of art, and their reverence for the spirit of antiquity; we may expect that they will ere long
illustrate as it deserves this portion of the history of their land.

I cannot here part with my reader, without
apologizing for the incompleteness, perhaps the
inaccuracy, of the following Notes. They were
the results of a hasty tour of a very few months,
collected originally without any view to publi-
cation; and are now printed in order that the
information, however trifling, being once collected,
may not immediately be lost. I shall consider
myself well rewarded, if they assist any one to
observe more thoroughly, or induce him to contribute any thing more complete.

NOTE.

THE nomenclature by which I have in the following Essay proposed to designate the kinds of vaults,
applies only to the simpler kinds of vaulting, which class
is what I have there had principally to describe; it
contains no provision for the representation of those
more complex roofs, which at a later period became so
frequent in this country. These roofs are commonly
called roofs of " fan-tracery," and are described by
Mr. Ware, in his Observations on Vaults, as " ribbed
vaults by ribs of the same curvature." It may, perhaps, be allowable here to mention the manner in which
I would propose to describe these, so as to keep in view
their connexion with those enumerated in the following
work.

Between two successive *transverse* cells in a groined
vault, (see p. 5.) the roof on each side of the building
consists of a mass in the form of an inverted curvilinear
pyramid or conoid, occupying the spandrels both of
the transverse and of the longitudinal vaults. This
space I will call the *spandrel-conoid:* and I shall employ this term, whether its form be horizontally circular or not. In common quadripartite vaulting, this
spandrel-conoid will have its horizontal section a rectangle at all heights from the bottom. Its concave

surfaces are the same as the surfaces of the longitudinal and transverse cells, the transverse ribs run along its surface, and the diagonal ribs along its edges.

The vaulting becomes *complex*, when the surface of the spandrel-conoid is subdivided by additional ribs or *veins** diverging from the top of the vaulting pillar. In this case the faces between these veins are often inclined to each other: the spandrel-conoid becomes a pyramid of many sides with a curvilinear slope, and its horizontal sections become polygons; and, by a change of the same kind, the surfaces become curvilinear, and the sections become circles.

In these kinds of vaulting the portions of the roof are concave to a person looking vertically upwards from the interior, and convex to a person looking horizontally. I would therefore call them both *concavo-convex* vaulting. The chapels of King's college at Cambridge, and of Henry the VIIth at Westminster, are instances of concavo-convex vaulting. The Lady-chapel at Wells is octagonal concavo-convex.

In both kinds, the ribs or veins which run along the surface of the conoids and diverge from the top of the vaulting pillar may be called *the diverging veins.* These diverging veins, especially in circular concavo-convex vaulting, are crossed at various distances from their origin by horizontal lines or circular bands, which may be referred to the point of divergence as their center; and these I will call *the concentric bands.* The

---

* The French have a convenient and expressive term for these lines,—" nervures."

spaces in the roof bounded by the diverging veins and the concentric bands, are *the pannels* of the vaulting.

The detail of the vaulting will depend upon the number and position of the diverging veins. In concavo-convex vaulting these may be described by stating *how many pannels* there are *on each side of the transverse rib*, with other peculiarities of decoration. In polygonal concavo-convex vaulting, we often have also shorter ribs *tying* together various points of the larger ones, (with ornaments or *bosses* at the junctions) and these *tye-ribs* are in some instances multiplied, so that the roof may be described as *covered with reticulating ribs*.

In all the concavo-convex roofs there occur between the bases of the spandrel-conoids certain spaces along the ridge of the main or longitudinal vault, which from their form I would call *the ridge-lozenges*. These often contain ornamental bosses, &c.

According to this nomenclature the roof of the Chapel of King's College, Cambridge, would be thus described. It has circular concavo-convex vaulting, with diverging veins, crossed by four concentric bands. The bands are ornamented with coronet points. The transverse ribs are large and prominent. The concentric spaces on each side the transverse rib are divided into twelve pannels (except the space contiguous to the top of the vaulting pillar, which has only six) and these pannels have cinque-foiled heads. The ridge-lozenges are feathered, and have large bosses, a rose and a portcullis alternately.

The singularly complex and artificial roof of Henry the Seventh's chapel at Westminster consists of circular conoids; the two lateral semi-conoids of each transverse section are (or *appear* to be) supported by the vaulting shafts; while the two intermediate conoids as well as that which occupies the ridge-lozenge, have no visible support, and appear as *pendents*. The roof is covered by an exquisite net-work of the veins and pannels which diverge from the points of these conoids. The real support of the roof are the transverse ribs which proceed from the intermediate pendent conoids to the wall, and are connected with the roof by a web of open tracery.

Note on Page 17.

It is here asserted, that no building of Norman architecture exists in England with the center aisle covered by original vaulting. It appears that there is an exception to this rule in the case of the Chapel of " the White Tower" in the Tower of London. This chapel has side aisles separated by massive Norman piers, and covered with Roman vaulting; but the center space is vaulted with a *cylindrical* stone vault, resting on the walls of the triforium ; the eastern termination being coved so as to accommodate the form to the semi-circular apsis of the chapel. The upper windows let in the light through the triforium arches. A room below the chapel is vaulted in the same manner, the spaces under the side aisles being, in this story, solid wall.

This tower is said to have been built by Gundulph, bishop of Rochester, in, or soon after, the year 1078.

CHAP. I.

OF THE CAUSES OF POINTED ARCHITECTURE.

SECT. 1. *Of the Romanesque and Gothic Styles.*

THE ancient churches of Europe offer to us two styles of architecture, between which, when we consider them in their complete developement, the difference is very strongly marked.

During the first thousand years of the Christian period, religious edifices were built in the *former* of these two styles. Its characters are a more or less close imitation of the features of Roman architecture. The arches are round; are supported on pillars retaining traces of the classical proportions; the pilasters, cornices and entablatures, have a correspondence and similarity with those of classical architecture; there is a prevalence of rectangular faces and square-edged projections; the openings in walls are small, and subordinate to the surfaces in which they occur; the members of the architecture are massive and heavy; very limited in kind and repetition; the enrichments being introduced rather by sculpturing surfaces, than by multiplying and extending the component parts. There is in this style a predominance of *horizontal* lines, or at least no predominance and prolongation of vertical ones. For

A

instance, the pillars are not prolonged in mouldings; the walls have no prominent buttresses, and are generally terminated by a strong horizontal tablet or cornice. This style may conveniently be designated by the term ROMANESQUE. The appellation has been proposed by Mr. Gunn, as implying a corrupted imitation of the Roman architecture: and though the etymological analogy according to which the word is formed, is perhaps not one of extensive prevalence, the expression seems less liable to objection than any other which has been used, and has the advantage of a close correspondence with the word *Romane*, which has of late been commonly employed by the French antiquarians to express the same style. This same kind of architecture, or perhaps particular modifications of it, have been by various persons termed Saxon, Norman, Lombard, Byzantine, &c. All these names imply suppositions with regard to the history of this architecture which it might be difficult to substantiate; and would, moreover, in most cases not be understood to describe the style in that generality which we learn to attribute to it, by finding it, with some variations according to time and place, diffused over the whole face of Europe.

The *second* style of which we have spoken, made its appearance in the early centuries of the second thousand years of the Christian world. It is characterized by the pointed arch; by pillars which are extended so as to lose all trace of classical proportions; by shafts which are placed side by side, often with different thicknesses, and are variously clustered and combined. Its mouldings, cornices and capitals, have no longer the classical shapes and members; square edges, rectangular surfaces, pilasters, and entablatures disappear; the elements of building become slender, detached, repeated and multiplied; they assume forms implying flexure and ramification. The openings become the principal part of the wall, and the other portions are subordinate to these. The universal tendency is to the predominance and prolongation of *vertical* lines; for instance, in the interior, by continuing the shafts in the arch-mouldings; on the exterior, by employing buttresses of strong projection, which shoot upwards through the line of parapet, and terminate in pinnacles.

All over Europe this style is commonly termed GOTHIC; and though the name has often been objected to, it seems to be not only convenient from being so well understood, but also by no means inappropriate with regard to the associations which it implies. That the Goths as a particular people had nothing to do with the establishment of the style in question, is so generally notorious, that there can be no fear of any one being, in that respect, misled by the term. The notion which suggested the use of the word was manifestly the perception, that the style under consideration was a complete deviation from, and contrast with, the whole principle and spirit of Roman architecture; and that this innovation and antithesis were connected with the course which taste and art took among the nations who overthrew the Roman empire, and established themselves on its ruins. And this is so far a true feeling of the origin and character of the new architecture, that we may consent to accept the word by which it has been thus designated, without being disturbed by the reflexion that those who first imposed this name, considered it as conveying the reproach of barbarism. We, indeed, should take a very different view from theirs of the merit and beauty of the new style. We should maintain, that in adopting forms and laws which are the reverse of the ancient ones, it introduced new principles as fixed and true, as full of unity and harmony, as those of the previous system; that these principles were applied with as extensive a command of science and skill, as great a power of overcoming the difficulties and effecting the ends of the art, as had ever been attained by Greek or Roman artists; and that they gave birth to monuments as striking, of as august and elevated a character, as any of which we can trace the existence in the ancient world. Our present business however is not with the merits, but the history, of the art.

The question of the causes of the transition from one of these styles to the other has been much agitated during the last half century. In the course of these discussions "the origin of the pointed arch" has generally been put forwards as the most important branch of the enquiry; a natural result of the common disposition to reduce a problem to the most definite and simple form. This is however an imperfect statement of the real question; for the pointed arch, far from being the single novelty in that change in architecture to which reference is made, is but one among a vast number of peculiarities which, taken altogether, make up the newer style: and this style would continue to exhibit a contrast with the one which preceded it, even if the round arch were used instead of the pointed one, as in some instances is actually the case.

Still, however, if we could shew with probability the reason which produced the prevalence of the pointed arch, this would be an important step in the history of the architectural revolution, and might throw much light on other parts of this history. Now we can point out a cause, which not only might possibly, but which must almost necessarily, have given rise to the general use of such arches; and it is one object of this Essay to illustrate this necessity, and the manner in which it affected ecclesiastical buildings.

The cause to which I refer, is the mode of VAULT-ING churches, and the instances in which I have been enabled to trace its operation, are the churches in the neighbourhood of the Rhine principally, and also in some other parts of the Continent.

SECT. 2. *Of the Origin of pointed Vaulting.*

The combination of vaults in the roof of a church is not easy to represent by figures, and hence there is some difficulty in conveying an exact conception of the contrivances which I have to describe. It may, however, perhaps be understood in the following manner.

In a vaulted church, we have in general one vault which runs longitudinally along the church; and the upper windows open into the sides of this longitudinal vault by shorter vaulted spaces, which, running perpendicularly to the length of the building, may be called *transverse* vaults. And the intersection of longitudinal and transverse vaults in this, and similar situations, would naturally lead to the introduction of pointed arches.

To make this evident, let us consider a single *compartment* of the church, that is, a portion of the center aisle (nave or choir) consisting of one arch, or one window in length, and of the breadth of the center aisle for its breadth. If this length and breadth be equal, such a compartment can be exactly vaulted over by means of semi-circular vaults intersecting each other, and strengthened by semi-circular arches, as is represented in Fig. 1. Each vault may be built exactly as if it were single; the two vaults will meet in an edge or groin of a regular elliptical form, lying diagonalwise across the compartment, and the lines running along the top of each vault will be horizontal lines. This kind of vaulting was practised by the Romans, and for the sake of brevity I shall call it *Roman vaulting*.

But the case will be different, if we suppose this equality of length and breadth no longer to subsist: if, for instance, the breadth of the window-space be smaller than the breadth of the aisle, as in Fig. 2. If, now, each of these breadths be vaulted over by semi-circular vaults, as in that figure, the transverse vault will not reach to the top of the longitudinal one, but will cut it obliquely in an irregular curve: the line running across the top from one window to its opposite, will be a broken line: the forms will be of some complexity to calculate, and can only be executed by great skill, and with much difficulty. This kind of vaulting is to be seen in modern buildings, for instance, in St. Paul's in London, but may be supposed not to have occurred as practicable to the architects of the middle ages.

If in this case, however, we suppose that the narrower space, (the window) is covered with a *pointed*

arch *of the same height* as the semi-circle, and with a
vault corresponding to this arch, the forms of the
vaulting become much easier both to determine and to
execute. The lines running along the top, both of the
longitudinal and of the transverse vaults, will again be
continuous horizontal lines ; and the edges formed by
the intersection of the two vaults will follow nearly,
but not exactly, the diagonals of the compartment. See
Fig. 3.

But if instead of supposing one of the vaults only to
have a pointed arch for its form, we suppose the longitudinal and transverse arches to be both pointed, and of
the same height (which is always possible, whatever be
the disproportion of the breadths) the arrangement will
become still more convenient. This is represented in
Fig. 4. All the divisions of the roof will be of similar
forms, and capable of being planned and executed in
a similar manner : and the edge or intersection of the
two vaults will be more nearly than before in the direction of the diagonal of the compartment, and will also
be nearly in the shape of a pointed arch, resembling the
original longitudinal and transverse arches.

If we erect, upon each diagonal of the compartment,
a pointed arch of the same height as the longitudinal
and transverse arches, the vault may, by a slight accommodation of the curvatures, be made exactly to fit this
arch. This arch, when marked by a projecting band of
stone, is called *a diagonal rib :* and this form of vaulting, with transverse and longitudinal pointed arches, and
with diagonal ribs, is the most simple and the most
prevalent form which occurs after the completion of
the architectural revolution.

8

It is not only that the forms and bearings of the parts in this arrangement are more easy and simple than in any other which suggests itself, capable of answering the same ends, but also its strength is more easily secured, and the mechanical construction of the vault much facilitated: the longitudinal, transverse, and diagonal ribs being probably first erected, and then the vaulting parts added, without the necessity of wooden *centers* covering the whole compartments.

This account is not proposed here as new. It is the theory which Mr. Saunders published in 1811, and which he has very ably and ingeniously explained in the 17th volume of the Archæologia*. In the same volume, Mr. Ware appears to be of a similar opinion, and the same view, or at least one nearly approaching to it, was taken of the subject by Mr. Essex, as appears by Mr. Kerrich's statement (*Archæologia*, Vol. XVI. p. 315.), and seems to be entertained with more or less distinctness by several continental antiquaries. My object is to illustrate the opinion somewhat further, by considering this part of the construction of a church in connexion with other portions of the edifice: and also to shew how the necessity which produced this change shews itself in various buildings in Germany and elsewhere.

It will be observed, that this theory of the origin of pointed arches must be considered as standing upon different ground from other theories which have been

---

* I may venture to observe, however, that the opinion which supposes Canterbury to be the first instance of pointed vaulting, appears to be untenable.

proposed, inasmuch as they only shew how the *form* of such an arch *may* have been suggested, not how the *use* of it *must* have become universal. The hypotheses which derive pointed arches from the intersections of branches of trees—or from the pointed form of doorways made by two stones leaning against each other — and even the very favourite opinion which supposes such arches to have originated with the intersecting round-headed arcades of the earlier architecture, must be considered as without value on this account. It is true, that, in these ways pointed arches would occur ; and so they would in many others; for instance, as has been observed, in proving the first Proposition of Euclid. But this *possible* construction of the pointed arch affords us no key to its adoption—does not explain to us why it grew into use, *rapidly* as to time ; *universally*, as to its application in all members of the building ; and *exclusively* as to the final rejection of the round arch previously employed, and of all the other forms, many of which would be as obviously suggested as this form of the pointed arch. Whereas, the theory which I am now to develope, pretends not only to shew how this arch *might* be invented ; but that it, or something like it, *must* have been wanted, discovered and employed.

That the adoption of this arch led to the other changes which combined to form the Gothic, is not capable of being proved with the same cogency; but yet we shall, it is hoped, be able to trace a natural and almost necessary influence of this element upon the other parts of the building, which seems to explain better than any other hypothesis the formation of the new style.

It will appear, I think, from what has already been said, that the vaulting of a space of which the length and breadth were different, could only be effected by abandoning the semi-circular arch. The forms which the vaulting assumed when this arch ceased to be exclusively employed, were various. They were, moreover, variously affected by the distribution of the other parts of the building, and I shall consider the consequence and progress of this combination of causes.

Sect. 3. *Of the Aisled Form of Churches.*

A circumstance in the arrangement of Christian Churches which very remarkably influenced the subordinate parts, was their distribution into a center aisle and two side aisles. Some may perhaps be disposed to trace this construction to a remoter origin. Something resembling it is indeed found in the religious edifices of very distant times and countries. The Egyptian temples of Ybsambul and Hermontis are separated by two rows of piers or pillars into three alleys. The division of the central from the lateral spaces by longitudinal rows of pillars, is found also in the Opisthodomos of the Parthenon at Athens, and seems to have been general in the hypæthral temples of the ancients, as for instance in that at Pæstum. In this very ancient temple, indeed, we have another remarkable approximation to the arrangement of a Christian Church, for we find over each of these inner rows another range of smaller pillars, exhibiting a striking resemblance to a clerestory.

Others may consider this form of Christian Churches as directly deduced from that of the Roman basilicæ, many of which are stated to have been applied to religious uses after the legal establishment of Christianity. These buildings consisted of two parallel ranges of covered porticos with an intervening space; and when this intervening space was covered in, obviously formed three aisles.

But, however this form may have originated, being once adopted as the usual construction of churches, it gave rise to many peculiarities, and determined most of the component parts of our ecclesiastical architecture.

The columns which separated the three aisles from each other became the *piers* of the church. These columns almost universally supported arches, which were generally used in the vaulting of the side aisles, and these are the *pier arches* of all aisled churches.

The center aisle was most frequently raised above the side aisles by walls resting upon the pier arches. The central elevated space was then lighted by windows pierced in this wall over the side aisles, and thus we have *clerestory windows*.

The side aisles were mostly vaulted with stone, and had over the stone roof a wooden one sloping upwards towards the clerestory. In this manner, a space necessarily intervenes between the top of the pier arches and the bottom of the clerestory windows. This space, when ornamented in the interior by a range of openings or pannels, became the *triforium*.

These different parts are seen in Fig. 6., which may be considered as the general type or pattern of two compartments of an aisled church*. The parts which have just been mentioned occupy in all complete churches the positions in which they are here drawn; and the differences in the form and decoration of these parts characterize the different successive styles.

But in order to see the whole effect of the triple arrangement, we must consider the manner in which the building was roofed.

Sect. 4. *Of the Kinds of Vaulting employed in Churches.*

Before we describe the combinations of vaults which occur in the roofs of churches, there are two kinds of simple vaults which must be mentioned.

No. 1. The *cylindrical* vault†, resting on the tops of the side walls with its axis in the longitudinal direction of the building. This is a very common and ancient mode of vaulting, but is rarely used to form the roofs of churches. It does not conveniently admit of clerestory windows, and is on that account ill-suited to such a purpose. There is, however, one part of many very early churches where it is constantly found, namely, in the roof of the compartment which intervenes between the *apsis*‡ of the church and the

---

* The triforium is here represented only by a blank space in the wall.

† This kind of ceiling is also occasionally called a wagon, barrel, tunnel, or cradle roof.

‡ The semi-circular or polygonal portion usual at the east end of the choir is so called. The same term is applied to a similar termination at the end of the transept or nave.

*crossing** of the transept. This compartment is also
generally different from the rest of the church in other
respects, and for the sake of compendious reference will
be called the *intermediate compartment.* It is covered
with a cylindrical vault at St. Aposteln, St. Martin,
St. George, and St. Mary Capitoline, all of them
churches existing, with many others of the most ancient
and curious construction, in the very remarkable city
of Cologne.

The cylindrical vault is found on a very large scale
in the ancient building called the Temple of Peace at
Rome. It occurs in many modern churches, of which
I may mention St. Peter's at Rome. It is not very
common in England, but is almost universal in the
churches of Cornwall, where each of the three aisles
is so roofed.

No. 2. In the ancient churches, the semi-circular
east end is the general form, and is covered with a plain
semi-dome: viz. the half of a hemisphere, smooth and
ribless. This domical apsis is usually somewhat lower
than the end of the choir to which it is attached; so as
on the outside to shew the gable wall of the choir above
the semi-circular termination. This semi-circular part
has also very uniformly a peculiar open gallery, and other
constant arrangements, outside; and the interior construction of the apse which has just been described is
equally constant in the oldest structures. Besides the
Cologne churches mentioned in the last paragraph, all

---

* The portion of the building which is over that space in the
ground plan where the transept crosses the nave is called the crossing.

of which have this form, we may adduce St. Gereon, St. Maurice, St. Cunibert, St. Pantaleon, in the same city; the great cathedrals of Mentz, Spires, and Worms; the great abbies of Laach near Andernach on the Rhine, and Eberbach near Elfeld in the Rheingau; and indeed almost all the churches of pure Romanesque character. Not only the choir, but the side aisles also have frequently this termination eastward; and this construction seems to be the earliest form of the church which we commonly find. This form is also very generally diffused, both in Normandy, and in Germany. To this prevalence Cologne, however, offers an exception. In that city four or five of the most ancient churches, which are formed into a group by their resemblances of style, have a plan in which, instead of this triple eastern apsis, we have apses at the *ends* of the transept, similar to that of the choir.

The combination of a center aisle with the side aisles introduced various methods of vaulting, which may be enumerated as follows:

No. 3. The simplest mode of vaulting *three* aisles is to make them all of the same height and width, the width being that of the pier arches; and to repeat the Roman vaulting for each square compartment thus produced.

This vaulting, with plain semi-circular bands, and no diagonal ribs, is found in many ancient buildings of small size, for instance, in the Ottmar-Capelle in the Burg at Nuremberg, and, with some modification, in the Margareten-Capelle, which is underneath the former chapel. It may be seen on a magnificent scale in the superb cellars of the ancient monastery of Eberbach in the Rheingau. In crypts it is extremely common both in Germany and in England; and in these cases is often repeated for more than three aisles, as at Canterbury, where it extends to five.

This mode of roofing is occasionally used in all the successive styles, the pointed arch being introduced instead of the round one, and the details altered accordingly. The Eucharius-Capelle at Nuremberg exhibits it with a mixture of round and pointed arches, belonging to the transition from one style to another. The Temple Church in London is a beautiful instance of the same arrangement in the style of the early English Gothic. The smaller of the two churches in the monastery of Eberbach just mentioned has a similar disposition, with the details of a still earlier pointed style. The mode of vaulting churches with three aisles of equal height was, however, most practised on a great scale at a considerably later period, when we have very large edifices of this construction with characters which imply a decline from the best Gothic style. Among many instances, I may mention St. Stephen at Vienna, St. Lefrau at Oberwesel, St. Stephen at Mentz, the cathedral at Frankfort, St. Martin at Landshut. The gigantic height of several churches thus built, the openness and lightness of them in consequence of the size and distribution of the windows, are circumstances which often make them impressive and imposing, in spite of the defects of their details and execution. They are generally conspicuous externally by an enormous height and breadth of slated or tiled roof, and by the absence of a clerestory.

No. 4.   In most churches, however, the center aisle is both higher and wider than the side aisles, and the building then requires a different mode of roofing.

The side aisles, being generally narrow, did not offer any considerable difficulty to the architect. They were built with a breadth nearly equal to the span of the pier arches, and then covered with equal intersecting semi-circular vaults on each compartment, according to the Roman vaulting described in Section 2. They had semi-circular vaulting bands across the aisle between each compartment, and generally had no diagonal ribs. The compartments of the vaults are very frequently more or less *domical** in their form.

Of the ways of covering the center aisle, the first which I shall mention, is to place a flat wooden roof upon this space. In this case, the roof may rest upon the level tops of the clerestory walls, and we have no occasion for any pillars at all in that part of the edifice. If, however, the wall is faced with pillars or pilasters, these run up to the top of the wall, and have their capitals at the wall-plate so as to support the beams; whereas, in walls intended for vaulting, the capitals of the vaulting pillars are necessarily much lower, so as to support the vaulting bands; in most instances they are nearly at the level of the bottoms of the clerestory windows.

In Fig. 6. the capitals are considerably below the top of the wall; but if the vault be removed, and a roof placed on the tops of the walls (the wall which is here

---

* That is, the intersection of the diagonal edges or ribs of each compartment is somewhat higher than the summits of the transverse and longitudinal arches by which the compartment is bounded.

drawn as imperfect being supposed to be completed to the same height as the opposite one) the capitals would naturally be carried to the summit of the wall.

This method of roofing large spaces seems in England to have been exclusively used during the prevalence of Norman architecture. I know no instance of a large center aisle of an Anglo-Norman building which possesses, or was intended to possess, a stone roof; and the above-mentioned position of the capitals clearly indicates the original design. Thus Peterborough, the nave of Ely, St. Peter's at Northampton, Steyning, Romsey, are calculated for flat roofs. In the latter church, even the nave, which is executed in the Early English style, has the same arrangement; probably for the sake of accommodation to the rest. The large buildings of Normandy of the earliest style in that province, have the same disposition; which obtains till we come to the two great Abbayes at Caen.

In Germany, as we shall shortly see, the art of vaulting large spaces seems to have been practised extensively, while in our country it was unknown. At the same time, however, that this was in use, many churches were built for flat roofs. Thus the abbey-church of Limburg on the Haardt, which was founded the same day as the neighbouring *vaulted* cathedral of Spires, is of the flat-roofed class. Other German churches of the same class which may be noticed, are Schwarzach near Rastadt; the Schotten-Kirche, the Obermünster Kirche, and the church of St. Emmeran, at Ratisbon; St. Burckardus at Würzburg; the church of Paulinerzelle in Thuringia; the old church at Schaffhausen in Switzerland; the churches at Ditkirchen on

B

the Lahn; at Ems on the same river; the ancient church on the Johannisberg; and, finally, St. Pantaleon and St. Cecilia at Cologne. In Italy this construction is still more common: the art of vaulting churches in stone in early times having been in that country far less practised than in Germany, if at all. Thus, St. Zeno at Verona and most of the old churches at Rome have flat roofs. In many of these Italian churches, the side aisles likewise are flat-roofed, which is the case also at Paulinerzelle: but in general, both in Germany and England, the side aisles, in such cases, are vaulted with Roman vaulting.

All the churches above-mentioned are of the most decidedly ancient and Romanesque character, and many of them highly curious. But this same mode of covering churches was resumed in later times, and in England is extremely common in that which Mr. Rickman terms the *Perpendicular* style; of which construction Great St. Mary's at Cambridge is a good instance.

No. 5. Instead of this wooden roofing, it is obvious that the architects would be tempted to extend to the center aisle the same art by which the side aisles were vaulted. Here however several difficulties offered themselves. The center aisle with its clerestory would have been altogether inadmissible without making it wider than the side aisles. If therefore it were covered with Roman vaulting, the distance of its pillars must be different from that of those in the side aisles, and thus the spaces, without some adjustment, would not correspond.

The artifice which was at first employed, and which forms our fifth method of roofing, was to make the

center aisle *twice* the width of the side aisles, and to
cover it with compartments of Roman vaulting, retaining the use of *semi-circular arches in both directions.*

By this means the pillars which supported the vaulting of the center aisle coincided with the *alternate* piers,
and the pier arches were distinguished into pairs. The
roof of the center aisle was divided into squares, by
transverse semi-circular ribs, springing from the pillars
which belonged to the alternate piers, and these pillars
had also semi-circular arches running longitudinally
from one to another along the clerestory wall. Each
compartment of the center aisle corresponded to two
compartments of the side aisles. See Fig. 6.

This mode of vaulting, with semi-circular arches
both ways, and with no diagonal ribs, is still found in
several ancient churches; though it has often been
replaced by more modern vaults. It is found with
considerable dimensions, in the churches of St. Maurice and St. George, at Cologne; the ancient monastery churches of Laach near Andernach and Eberbach
near Elfeld; and on a still grander scale in the gigantic
cathedral of Spires, where the span of the vault is
about 45 feet; and though the storms of war have so
often and so fiercely burst upon this city, it is con-
fidently asserted by the most learned antiquaries, that
part of the vaulting is of its original form. In most
of these instances, and especially at Spires, the compartments are considerably *domical*, the intersection of
the diagonals being higher than the summits of the
bounding arches. The above instances of Roman vaulting are, however, far inferior in magnitude to those
executed by the Romans themselves. The great hall

in the baths of Diocletian, now the church of S. Maria degli Angioli, has a span of 67 feet, and the vaulting of the Temple of Peace at Rome is said to have extended as far as 83 feet*.

This arrangement produced some peculiarities in the members of the building which deserve notice.

a. The alternate distinction of the piers is variously marked in buildings of this class. The *principal piers*, or those which possess vaulting pillars†, being generally more massive and important; and very often altogether different from the *intermediate piers*. The observations which are to be made on this subject apply to some of the other modes of vaulting hereafter to be described, and will be best illustrated by the notice of examples.

Mentz, Spires and Worms are three colossal buildings belonging to the systems now under consideration Mentz has plain *pilaster masses‡* for the intermediate piers, while the principal piers have in front of the pilaster a vaulting shaft rising from the floor to the vault. Worms has the same arrangement, except that the vaulting pillar instead of a simple shaft is a pilaster with a shaft in front of it. Spires, the vaulting of which is the greatest example of this fifth mode, has pilasters faced with shafts, in two stories, for the principal pier, while the intermediate pier has a shaft which runs from the floor to the clerestory uninterrupted.

In several of the ancient churches of Cologne, this alternation is differently marked. In St. George, the

---

* Ware. Archæologia, Vol. xvii. p. 47.

† The pillars which run up to the clerestory, and support the vaulting of the center aisle, are called *vaulting pillars*.

‡ Rectangular pillars or portions of wall, with impost mouldings.

vaulting pillars are columns in front of pilaster masses, while the intermediate piers are columns* with cushion capitals †. In this case, however, the compartment of the center aisle corresponds not to 2, but to $2\frac{1}{2}$ of the compartments of the side aisles. At St. Maurice the intermediate piers are low pilaster masses, the vaulting pillars tall pilasters. St. Cunibert, in a later style, has the same difference. At St. Aposteln the intermediate piers have the impost moulding at the sides, but not in front; the vaulting pillars are half columns from the floor. At St. Andrew, the intermediate pier has a pilaster mass of some width, with half columns in the sides, supporting the pier arches.

In the transition style, where the triforium is a prominent feature, the vaulting pillars alone run up to the clerestory, the intermediate piers being low masses, as at Andernach, Sinzig, Boppart, and the churches at Coblentz.

As we advance to later examples, these differences become more complicated; consisting often in a greater number or different form of shafts and mouldings in the alternate piers, as at Bamberg, Limburg on the Lahn.

---

* I shall use the term *columns* exclusively for pillars possessing some approximation to the effect of classical proportions; *shafts*, for those which are too slender and long to have such an effect. Pillar is a comprehensive term including all such upright members.

† The capitals which I have distinguished by this term are extremely common in Romanesque work both in England and in Germany. They consist of large cubical masses projecting considerably over the shaft of the column, and rounded off at the lower corners. Sometimes they are cleft below, so as to approach in form to two or more such round-cornered masses. They may be considered as rude imitations of the very projecting ovolo and thick abacus which compose the capital of the Grecian Doric.

This alternation of the piers is seldom found in England. It is, however, to be seen at Canterbury, with that kind of vaulting which we shall call *sexpartite*, and at Durham, where it occurs associated with a kind of vaulting shortly to be described, in which the cause of the alternation is almost obliterated.

b. *The distribution of the clerestory windows* is also affected by this style of vaulting. The obvious construction was to put one such window in the arch-space of each arched compartment of the clerestory wall. But it was also usual to have a window in each compartment of the side aisles. According to this arrangement, therefore, the clerestory windows would only be half as numerous as those of the aisle, and would fall between the alternate pairs of the latter.

This is the case in some churches vaulted in the manner now described, but, in general, the light thus afforded, with the small windows then in use, was not sufficient; and attempts were made in various ways to remedy the inconvenience. One of the most common was to place *two* clerestory windows in each compartment of the wall under the transverse vault; and these windows were necessarily near each other, in order that they might be under the middle and highest part of each arch. In this way, the clerestory windows are in pairs, and though equal in number to the aisle windows, do not lie over them. And the occurrence of the vaulting in double compartments may be discerned outside, from this arrangement of the clerestory windows at alternately greater and less intervals. See Fig. 6.

The former arrangement of windows is found at Laach, though the vaulting in this case is in single compartments. At Bamberg we have it with alternate blank windows outside the clerestory, for the sake of regularity. The other distribution obtains very generally in churches vaulted according to this method, and to the one next to be described. Thus in the cathedrals at Mentz, Spires, and Worms, the clerestory windows are in pairs. The same is the case in St. Martin's at the latter place—in the abbey at Eberbach—in the churches at Sinzig and at Andernach on the Rhine, and in St. Maurice at Cologne. I do not know that it occurs any where in England, except in the side aisles of the choir at Durham.

No. 6. We have now to notice cases where the vaulting is modified. by the introduction of the pointed arch. And, in the first place, where *the transverse ribs* only are pointed*, the *longitudinal* ones being, as before, semi-circular, and each compartment of the center aisle still answering to two in the side aisles. This vaulting is not, at first sight, much different from the preceding kind. It varies however in this, that the breadth of the center aisle is no longer necessarily double of that of the side aisles; and also in almost always possessing *diagonal ribs*, which the preceding vaulting in general has not. The alterations of the other members of the architecture which begin to make their appearance along with these and the succeeding changes of vaulting, must be described afterwards. What was said in the last article of the alternation of the piers, and of the distribution of the clerestory windows applies here also.

---

* The arches which form projecting strips on the surface of the vaulting are called *ribs*; those which run in the direction of the length being called *longitudinal,* and those which run across the length, *tranverse.*

Mentz is the greatest example of this kind of vaulting. St Paul at Worms, the church at Andernach, are other instances: the cathedral at Trent is also of this class. In St. Aposteln at Cologne, the transverse ribs are semi-circular, the vaulting being of a kind hereafter to be mentioned; but, commonly, when one of the bands only is pointed, it is the transverse one.

No. 7. The next step in the order of change, is that where both *the longitudinal and transverse bands are pointed.* We have here universally diagonal ribs, and this is by far the most common vaulting in all churches belonging to times after the invention of the pointed vault. It is capable of any proportion of length and breadth, and, in its later form, generally includes lengthways only one compartment of aisle. In the early form however which we have more particularly now to consider, it often contains two compartments, and two clerestory windows, arranged as in the two former cases.

Spires, Mentz, and Worms, the three great Romanesque cathedrals, form a progression with regard to vaulting which illustrates the divisions now explained; at Spires the arches are circular both ways; at Mentz the transverse one is pointed, the longitudinal being round; at Worms both are pointed. The church of St. Martin at Worms is vaulted exactly as the cathedral. Bamberg cathedral is an excellent specimen of the same kind; as are the transepts at Gelnhausen and Sinzig, and the nave at Bonn. St. Ambrose and Santa Maria delle Grazie at Milan may also be mentioned.

When, quitting the transition style, we come to the completely formed Gothic, we find in all countries where that architecture prevails, numberless instances of this mode of vaulting. The nave of Salisbury cathedral is a good simple example of it. In England the vaulting subsequently became complicated and varied with a much greater number of parts; but in Germany this kind of plain pointed vaulting is continued without any additional ribs into the period of the richest and most complete Gothic work, for instance, at Freyberg in the Brisgau. It may be observed, that in the German vaulting, the parts which have been above described have seldom even the longitudinal rib along the top of the vault which is so common in England.

No. 8. Another kind of vaulting which seems to be as early, or very nearly so, as that just described, and which is very frequent and characteristic, is what I shall call *sexpartite vaulting*. It will be necessary to explain the construction of this and the related classes of vaults.

In the kinds of vaults hitherto described, we have had four hollow spaces or *cells* diverging from the intersection of the diagonal ribs. These cells, which were round or cylindrical in the Roman vaulting, were pointed in the kind last described. This species of vaulting may be called *quadripartite*. If, now, we conceive a compartment which has two pointed clerestory windows on each side, and suppose, from the center of the longitudinal vault of this compartment, oblique pointed vaults to diverge to each of the four windows, we shall have the compartment covered with a roof consisting of six cells, which may be called, therefore, *sexpartite*. We have in this case six ribs diverging from the intersection; namely, the halves of two diagonals, and of the transverse rib between the pair of windows; besides which the compartment is bounded by transverse bands at each end. See Fig. 5.

This mode of vaulting is exceedingly common in early German churches, invariably accompanied by characters which imply that the transition from the Romanesque architecture is already in progress. St. Cunibert at Cologne is a good instance, and St. Aposteln was so, till the vaulting was altered a few years ago. In the latter instance, as has already been noticed, the transverse arches are circular, which is not common. Other examples are, Limburg on the Lahn, Sinzig, St. Sebaldus at Nuremberg, and a part of Bamberg cathedral. This species of vaulting is found in England in the choir at Canterbury, and though somewhat distorted, in the chapel of the Nine Altars at Durham. The nave at Lincoln has compartments of sexpartite vaulting*. St. Stephen at Caen is thus vaulted, and the contemporary Abbaye aux Dames is constructed in the same manner, except that each pair of windows is covered, not by two arches, but by two half-arches, separated by a vertical wall.

No. 9. In the same way in which we speak of quadripartite and sexpartite vaulting, we may also speak of *octopartite* vaulting, when we have eight cells diverging from a common point. This is a mode very commonly employed in vaulting the towers which occur at the crossing of the transept. It may be employed either *on a square base*, each side of the square being divided

---

* The choir of Lincoln has a most peculiar combination of vaults, which, to correspond with the nomenclature in the text, might perhaps be called *alternately semiquadripartite.*

into two halves; or *on an octagon base.* The square made by the transept's crossing the nave is often converted into an octagon by arches thrown over the corners, and then the latter kind of octopartite vaulting is employed: for instance at St. Aposteln; in the cathedrals at Mentz, (the western tower), Worms and Spires; in the churches at Gelnhausen, Limburg, Sinzig; and many others.

St. George de Bocherville in Normandy has a tower with octopartite vaulting on a square base: so also Lincoln.

It is very usual to vault the ends of the transept with a roof, of which the compartment towards the nave belongs to the quadripartite, and the other three quarters to the octopartite form; this occurs at Seligenstadt.

No. 10. The vaulting of the polygonal east apse is most commonly half (or rather $\frac{5}{8}$) of an octopartite compartment. In this case the cells are often very acute, as at Gelnhausen, Bamberg, Limburg, Mentz, Worms, &c. sometimes having windows in the escutcheon-shaped end of the cell.

SECT. 5. *Order of Succession of the Kinds of Vaulting.*

All the kinds of vaults above enumerated are found abundantly exemplified in the ancient churches of Germany: and there cannot be much doubt as to the order in which they began to be employed. This order may be inferred from two circumstances: the construction of the vaults themselves, and the accompanying details of the architecture; and the two determinations agree in a remarkable manner. And though much difficulty and uncertainty attends the historical investigation of the dates of the parts of buildings from external evidence, it appears that the testimony of historical writers, as far as we have it, is quite consistent with the inferred succession of inventions. It is to be observed, however, that though we may with tolerable certainty collect from internal evidence the *order* of these modes of vaulting, we cannot in this way determine any thing with regard to the *date* of each.

The oldest forms of vaulting which remain to us, are the two first enumerated; Nos. 1 and 2; the cylindrical for the choir, and the domical for the apsidal end; and this is the vaulting of St. Mary Capitoline at Cologne, a building which is asserted to be certainly of the eighth century; and of no less than five or six other churches of great antiquity in the same city. The cylindrical vault possesses no clerestory windows; and it is unfortunate that no nave remains of the date of the above buildings to show us how the earliest builders arranged that part of the edifice.

The oldest complete church-vaulting, therefore, is No. 5, the Roman vaulting of the center aisle, and this is employed in Germany at a period when the Normans and English did not vault large spaces, but covered them in the way described as No. 4. I shall not attempt to draw any inference from this difference: but it may be noticed, that one advantage which the Colognese possessed for the construction of vaults, was the extremely light and durable volcanic tuf which occurs in their neighbourhood, and of which the surfaces of their vaults are composed : the ribs both in this and in the preceding styles of vaulting being of harder stone.

The three great Romanesque cathedrals of the Upper Rhine offer, as has been said, a graduated progression of the earliest forms of cross vaulting, Nos. 5, 6 and 7, and it is scarcely possible, on considering the details and connexion of their members, to believe these vaults to be any other than original. These cathedrals, as to their earliest parts, were all built about the year 1000, or soon after, and a great number of other churches offering the same forms of vaulting claim the same date.

The *sexpartite* vaulting, No. 8, succeeded along with No. 7, to the earlier forms ; it is never however found without the indications of a later style than the one just mentioned. The quadripartite vaulting with one window in each compartment is in the same manner manifestly later than the vaulting like that of Worms, where though both arches are pointed, the clerestory windows are still in pairs.

It has been said, that associated with the kinds of vaulting last explained, we find innovations in the other elements of the architecture. What these alterations are, and how they seem to have been produced by the previous introduction of the pointed arch, we must now endeavour to explain.

SECT. 6.   *Influence of the Pointed Arch on other Parts of the Architecture.*

The following is proposed as a theory of the way in which the use of the pointed arch led to the general principle of Gothic architecture, and thus, in the course of time, altered and transformed all the subordinate parts.

The leading and predominant lines of Grecian and Roman architecture are horizontal, and this principle continues to have a considerable sway in the Romanesque style.

One result of the operation of this principle is, that the arch lines in this style are looked upon as having an analogy with the horizontal members. The tablets which follow the arch are considered as a kind of entablature. They are called the *architrave* of the arch ; they consist of the fascias and mouldings of the horizontal architrave; at its summit the arch is horizontal, and the face of the wall is considered as the frieze of its architrave. The vaulting ribs of Romanesque buildings are flat and square-edged like the horizontal elements.

But as soon as ever the pointed arch makes its appearance, this aspect begins to change. The diagonal ribs of pointed vaults are never flat and square-edged like the vaulting ribs of the Romanesque. *Rolls*, or bent cylinders, constitute these lines. At the same time the transverse ribs themselves begin to have their square edges formed into beads or smaller rolls; in a short time the flat part vanishes and the square rib becomes a roll. It then becomes a cluster of rolls, then a cluster of mouldings ; and when the change is advanced so far, parts of the cluster may separate and ramify, and assume any of the endless forms of Gothic architecture.

Now this change seems to be clearly connected with the adoption of the pointed arch. When that step is once made, the attribution of a horizontal character to the arch line necessarily ceases. It has no longer a horizontal summit, or an uninterrupted path from one point to another in the same horizontal line. Its form manifestly indicates an upward direction. It thus loses its correspondence with any part of the entablature, and we are naturally led to refer the arch line to the supporting pillar; to consider it as a continuation of this, and to give it that cylindrical form which implies such an origin.

This tendency being once admitted, the rest of the change proceeds by a still more obvious connexion. The pillars being thus conducted beyond the capital, we lose all perception of a limitation of them in the direction of their length : they may be produced in extent and diminished in thickness as much as we chuse; their capitals must no longer be square so as to stop them by a marked rectangular interruption : the common tendency of two shafts to prolong themselves indefinitely upwards, makes it natural to place them in contact; to form them into clusters; to combine them into groups, and to take up again in the arch mouldings the members of this group   And after this has been done, the formation of those flexible and upward-tending lines into the tracery of roofs, and all the varied forms of the richest Gothic work proceeds by a gradation which it is agreeable to trace, but unnecessary to detail.

But while this change of character takes place in the frame-work of a Gothic building, a similar progression may be considered as going on in the openings. When the clerestory windows have become pointed, they share the tendency of the rest of the edifice towards upward prolongation. To construct buildings in which this tendency operates, the architects adopted the excellent mechanical contrivance of strongly projecting buttresses. These were further improved into flying buttresses; and furnished with these admirable imple-plements, the architects of the complete Gothic style seem to have delighted in lifting to an immense height in the air the most gigantic and magnificent clerestories, enclosed by enormous areas of transparent wall. In this way are constructed and suspended the magical structures of Amiens, Strasburg, Freyberg, Cologne, and in the neighbourhood of the latter, the exquisite abbey-church of Altenburg. Sometimes, indeed, the architect " magnis excidit ausis"—attempted more than he could execute; as in the instance of Beauvais, splendid even in its failure; where the unexampled height and boldness of the clerestory were imposed on a lower story, which was found too weak for its task, and has since been relieved by interpolating a new pier in each interval of the old ones.

Such was the completion of the architectural revolution. The peculiarities of the German churches offer to us a confirmation of this account of its rise and progress; and at the same time seem to shew that the direct operation of the causes of the new architecture is to be sought rather in Germany than in our own country.

For it is worthy of notice, that in the churches of the Rhine, the pointed arch makes its appearance in the vaulting before it affects any other part, and is used to roof buildings in which all the other arches and openings are round: whereas in England, the struggle between the round and pointed styles seems to be carried on in all parts of the architecture at once, giving rise to most curious mixtures and combinations, and seeming to be the result of caprice and indecision rather than of any general cause.

It would be too much to say that we can trace the effect of the causes above indicated in all the novelties of detail which occur in the passage from the Romanesque style. Many, however, of these innovations are easily referred to the general spirit of the change now described ; and it is conceived that the succeeding Chapter, which contains the characters of the transition style, will further illustrate the formation of the complete Gothic.

C

CHAP. II.

———

SECT. 1.   *Difference of the Early English and Early
German Styles.*

THE observations just made apply only to the instances where the change of architecture is completed,
and in these the style of the German buildings resembles very exactly what Mr. Rickman has called the
Decorated English Style.   But there is a large class of
buildings in Germany constructed during the period
which elapsed while this change was still in progress;
and these buildings exhibit features somewhat different
from any of those styles which we find in England.
The architecture which in England immediately succeeded the Romanesque or Norman, has been called
the *Early English* style; and though it may be doubt-
ful whether the first steps which carried architects
beyond the Romanesque were made in England, it
seems to be certain that the Early English style as
it exists at Salisbury, for instance, was not developed
in the same manner in Germany, and is not in its most
characteristic shape to be found in that country *.

———

* The differences between the styles in England and Germany
which have the nearest correspondency, is by no means confined to
the transition style.   The Romanesque of Germany, which German
writers

That the English and the German architects beginning from the same point—the Romanesque, and arriving at the same result—the Decorated or Complete Gothic, should have gone by different roads, and made the transition each through a separate style, is a curious circumstance, and worthy of illustration. As the intermediate style in England has been called Early English,

---

writers often call Byzantine, varies in several respects from the Romanesque of England, which we have been habituated to term Norman. Thus we never find in the German churches the ponderous cylindrical piers which we have at Durham, Malmesbury, Steyning, &c.: we have not there the piers carved and channeled as is so frequent with us; (a few exceptions, such as the crypt of St. Gereon, hardly disturb this rule.) The German buildings have not the deep rich succession of mouldings to which we are accustomed in the door and pier arches; the latter, especially, are in Germany universally quite plain. The Romanesque of that country does not exhibit the extraordinary multiplicity and fantastical variety of mouldings and ornaments which so distinguishes our Norman—the *beak-head*, the *embattled fret*, &c. are hardly or not at all known. The *zig-zag* and the *triple-billet*, however, are used very prodigally in certain parts of German churches. The complete Gothic, of Cologne cathedral and Oppenheim for instance, coincides very nearly with our best Gothic of the 14th century; the *decorated* style of Mr. Rickman with *geometrical tracery*. The German buildings are generally purer and plainer in their details than ours, and the absence of dripstones is a remarkable difference. The tall clerestory and polygonal east end form very characteristic parts of the appearance of German buildings of this class.

The complete Gothic which is thus attained alike in England and Germany, is found with the same features in France, as in St. Ouen at Rouen.

After this general coincidence, the styles of different European nations seem again to diverge; the beautiful Perpendicular or Tudor architecture which was so much cultivated with us, being quite different from the contemporaneous or corresponding styles of France, Germany, and the Netherlands; and these again apparently being different from each other. And in these different paths the different countries seem to have gone on till the introduction of Italian or the revival of Classical architecture.

I shall call the intermediate style in Germany the *Early German;* and the following pages will be employed in an endeavour to characterize it, which so far as I know has not yet been attempted. I shall, for this purpose, point out its differences from the preceding or Romanesque style, for the differences between it and the complete Gothic are more obvious. The general character of the style is rather Romanesque than Gothic, though it has pointed arches and various other Gothic elements. The general character of the Early English on the other hand is decidedly Gothic; and, indeed, it cannot be considered otherwise than as a fully developed Gothic style.

To a person who has made himself acquainted with the Early English style, the differences which the Early German presents are very obvious. They have in common their slender shafts, clustered and banded, their pointed arches, and their mode of vaulting; but we do not commonly find in the interior of the transition churches of Germany the circular cluster of shafts, — the arches moulded into a broad and deep mass of small rolls with deep hollows between,—the circular abacus with its rounded upper edge,—the single lancet-headed windows, tall and narrow,—and the peculiar line of open flowers which is used so profusely in all Early English work. Nor do we observe on the outside the dripstone to the window,—the moulded or shafted window-sides *,

---

* The edge of the window opening when sloped or broken into mouldings, cannot, in Gothic work, be properly called the architrave. It is frequently necessary to mention it, and I have for this purpose used the term *window-side* in a fixed technical sense.

—the projecting buttress with its chamfered edge and triangular head,—the pyramidal pinnacles,—of our early cathedrals. What the elements are which we have in this style in Germany, will appear by the following description; and for the purpose of exhibiting the characters of Early German churches, I shall consider their parts in the following order: the Plan, the General Outline; the Vaulting; the parts of the Interior; and of the Exterior.

SECT. 2. *Characteristic Details of Transition or Early German Architecture.*

I. THE PLAN.

The *Plan* of the church in the Early German, as in the Romanesque style, consists principally of three aisles, of which the center one constitutes the nave and choir, and has a polygonal or semi-circular apse at its east end. In considerable buildings we have also generally a transept, and various other chapels for altars, besides the eastern altar. A difference observable in these points is, that in the older style the apse is generally semi-circular, in the transition style it is polygonal. In the old churches the eastern sides of the north and south transepts were formed in like manner into semi-circular apses (as in the old church on the Johannisberg, in the ruined church of St. Peter at Gelnhausen, and in the abbey church at Laach). And though in the succeeding style also it is common to have chapels on the east of the transept, end, these have seldom a simple semi-circular form; but have sometimes an additional recess, as at Gelnhausen and Sinzig; or some other form, as at Limburg; or disappear along with the transept, as at Bamberg, Andernach, and Boppart.

We have already had occasion to mention another arrangement very common in the early churches, and especially in those of Cologne, viz. that in which each end of the transept is formed as an apse (for instance, St. Mary Capitoline, St. Aposteln, St. Martin, &c.) And this also is occasionally imitated in the transition style, still substituting a polygonal for a semi-circular end, as at Bonn, and at Marpurg, if the latter be not too late to be here introduced. It is remarkable, that we find in many churches a round apse in one part, and polygonal ones in other parts. Thus at Bonn the end of the choir is circular, of the transepts angular. Here also may be mentioned instances such as those of Mentz, Worms, and Bamberg, where we have an apse at each end, round at the east, and angular at the west: the latter being in all these cases, as well as in the western apse of St. Sebaldus at Nuremberg, of the style now described.

In such cases of an eastern and western apse, we have also generally a western as well as an eastern transept, as at Mentz: and this second transept is found in several other churches, mostly Romanesque ones; as St. Aposteln, St. Andrew, St. Pantaleon at Cologne; St. Paul at Worms; the Schotten-kirche at Nuremberg. St. Cunibert has likewise a western transept.

The towers in many of the churches of the earliest style are near the east end. In the transition style it is very common to have towers both at the east and west, as at Bamberg, Andernach, Bonn, Arnstein, Limburg.

The latter, indeed, according to the plan, would have had two towers at the west end of the nave, and two smaller ones at each end of the transept, besides the central octagonal tower which it has in common with Gelnhausen, Seligenstadt, Sinzig, Heimersheim, and Bonn.

II. The General Outline.

The *general outline* of the church must depend principally upon its towers. If we suppose the great cathedrals of Mentz, Spires, and Worms, to be executed according to the original plan, which seems to be preserved to us in the form of the church of Laach, it would appear that the complete type of a large church consisted of four towers, (the two pairs having different forms and magnitudes,) and of two cupolas or pyramids. We see probably one of the best external elevations of such cupolas in the graceful octagonal pyramid of St. Aposteln. In this manner the outline of a single cathedral would present a group of edifices, clustered and varied like the view of a fine city. We see a specimen of the effect of such a group at Laach, just mentioned; where the deserted abbey church, standing with its six towers on the banks of the remarkable lake of that name, is a highly picturesque object*. Mentz has a striking appearance, but is somewhat spoiled by the inappropriate restorations which it has undergone. Worms is another instance of a group of towers. This complexity of outline does not appear to have been imitated by the architects of the transition style; and

---

* A sketch of this church is given in Plate 3.

in their buildings we have either two pairs of towers, as at Andernach, Bamberg, and Arnstein; or a center spire with a pair of towers; either eastern towers as at Gelnhausen, and we may add St. Cunibert at Cologne; or more generally western towers, as at Limburg, Bonn, Sinzig, Heimersheim, Seligenstadt; though the two first have smaller turrets besides. Boppart has two, and Bacharach one western tower only—at least remaining. The subordination of the lateral to the central towers in the group where that configuration is found, and the perspective combinations of the two pairs, in churches with four towers, produce a very pleasing effect in these buildings when perfect.

The towers of the Early German style, as well as of the Romanesque, have generally their sides terminated by pediments. It appears to be generally true, that in the earlier style these pediments have the angle at the summit nearly a right angle, and the horizontal, as well as the inclined cornices, strongly marked. In the later towers the pediment is more acute, and the cornice lighter. Sometimes, as at St. Martin and St. Cunibert, the tops are horizontal.

III.   The Vaulting.

The kinds of vaulting used in the churches of Germany have already been described in Chapter I, and we have noticed the order in which they succeeded each other. It will be sufficient to remind the reader, that the cylindral intermediate compartments (No. 1.), and domical east end (No. 2.), belong to the oldest Romanesque buildings—that the Roman vaulting

(No. 3.), is used for crypts and for side aisles —
that in the oldest Romanesque buildings, we have over
the center aisle either flat roofs (No. 4.), or large
Roman vaulting (No. 5.); that this vaulting becomes
pointed, either in the transverse direction (No. 6.), or
in both directions (No. 7.), the compartments being
still *double*, and the rest of the members continuing
to be of a Romanesque character.

These latter species of vaulting are used also when
the transition in the other members is already very
manifest, as at Andernach, Bamberg, &c. The sexpartite vaulting (No. 8.), and the vaulting (No. 7.) with
single compartments, belong more decidedly, however,
to the transition style. At St. Cunibert at Cologne
a great part of the work much resembles the Romanesque
churches in the same city; the plain round pier arches
rest on pilaster masses, the east end is a semi-dome, &c.
But the vaulting is sexpartite, with cells slightly pointed;
and accordingly we find other innovations: viz. the quadripartite vaulting of the side aisles has diagonal ribs;
the vaulting pilasters have slender shafts at their sides;
the shafts between the upper windows in the apse are
three-clustered; the aisle windows are many-foiled semi-
circles; and the clerestory windows much larger than in
the pure Romanesque buildings. And in the same
manner we may trace in other churches a variation of
the subordinate elements accompanying the newer kinds
of vaulting. We may particularly observe the flat and
square-edged vaulting-ribs of the pure Romanesque,
first acquiring roll edges, and finally becoming curved
mouldings, as has already been noticed in Sect. 5. of
Chap. I.

The round east end so generally characteristic of Romanesque churches, where we have a domical apse lower than the choir, is, in the transition style, exchanged for a polygonal form; and is vaulted with diverging cells, and raised to the same height as the roof of the choir, (vaulting, No. 10.). It is remarkable, that in the cathedrals at Mentz, Worms, and Bamberg, the eastern apse is domical and ribless, while the western one has octopartite vaulting with pointed cells. The west end of St. Sebaldus at Nuremberg is vaulted in the latter way; as are the east ends of Gelnhausen, Limburg on the Lahn, Seligenstadt, Sinzig, and the transept ends of Bonn. This vaulting of the apse is also retained in the complete Gothic style, and has certainly great beauty.

The octopartite vaulting is also often used in the transition style to cover the crossing of the transept; or the octagonal tower which rises from it, as at Seligenstadt, Gelnhausen, Limburg, the western parts of Mentz and Worms, &c.

Sometimes, however, we have in such a situation a dome with octopartite ribs, as at Sinzig, and at Heimersheim, about a league further up the Ahr. This vaulting occurs also in the choir at Seligenstadt. We have the octopartite vaulting with a quadripartite cell next the crossing, in the transepts of the latter church, also in the transepts of Limburg and of St. Cunibert, and the organ loft of Bacharach. The nave of Boppart is peculiar, its vaulting being a succession of domes on square bases, which have sixteen-partite ribs; but here perhaps, the walls were originally built for a flat roof.

The octopartite vaulting is used, as has been said, to cover an *octagonal tower*; and in the cases where such a feature exists, it is proper to notice the manner in which it is *set on* upon the square, (generally the crossing of the transept) which is its basis. A mode of making the junction which appears to belong to the earliest style (though not exclusively) is seen in St. Aposteln at Cologne: the sides of the octagonal tower which correspond to the angle of the square basis, and consequently project over them, are connected with these angles by a portion of a concave ribless surface or *concha*, such that the main longitudinal and transverse arches which support the tower, and the upper boundary of this concha, form a sort of spherical triangle. The eastern cupolas of Mentz, Worms and Spires, the center towers of Seligenstadt and Gelnhausen, are constructed in the same manner.

But in the Early German churches there is another mode of supporting those octagonal towers, which seems to belong more peculiarly to the transition style, of which the western cupolas of Mentz, Worms, and the tower of Limburg are examples. In these cases the concha above-mentioned is hollowed, so that its upper boundary forms an arch in the side of the octagonal tower. These arches have well-marked mouldings; and along with them we have corresponding arches in the other sides of the octagon, shafts in its angles, and other decorations which did not appear in the former method of erecting such towers.

IV. Interior.

I will next consider the *separate members of the interior*, taking them in this order: the piers and pier arches; the triforium; the clerestory; the side walls and windows; and the peculiarities which occur in the choir and transept.

1. *Piers and Pier Arches.*

The *principal*, or vaulting *piers* in the Romanesque style were often engaged columns, as at Laach, St. Mary Capitoline, St. Gereon, and St. Aposteln at Cologne; and as they are found in the aisles of a great number of churches, for instance, St. Andrew, St. Pantaleon, St. Maurice at Cologne, the church at Ems, and many others. In other instances, the vaulting pillars were pilasters, springing from the ground as in St. George and St. Maurice; or from the impost as at St. Ursula, and in the desecrated church of Eberbach, &c.

If we examine large Romanesque buildings, at Spires we find one column upon another, the upper capitals being of a very classical model. At Mentz the tall shaft is used alone. At Worms the pillar is too tall to be called a column, and has pilaster edges on each side. These three colossal cathedrals are remarkable for the simplicity of their parts.

When we approach the Early German style, we seldom find columns and pilasters approaching to classical proportions, in the situation now spoken of, and the alterations, though gradual, are very various.

We have pilasters with shafts at the sides, at Sinzig, Bonn, and St. Cunibert; advancing still by a repetition of these parts, we have often an assemblage of *engaged shafts and pier edges**, as at Limburg, Seligenstadt, Andernach, Bamberg; and sometimes triple shafts alone, as at Bacharach. In many instances, where the vaulting of this style has been added to an earlier building, we have vaulting shafts, clustered or single, springing from a corbel, or, more generally, from an end hooked into the wall above the impost. This occurs at St. Mary Capitoline, and St. Martin, in the nave, and is, indeed, very common.

Between the principal piers occur the *intermediate piers*, and these either send up no vaulting shafts at all, as in the three great cathedrals just mentioned, and in quadripartite vaulting on a smaller scale, for instance, St. Andrew, Cologne: or in sexpartite vaulting they supply vaulting shafts smaller and less important than the principal piers, as in St. Cunibert, St. Aposteln, Limburg and Bacharach, where these intermediate vaulting shafts spring from the *triforium tablet†*. These intermediate piers in large Romanesque buildings are tall pilaster-formed masses with imposts; as at Mentz, Spires and Worms, where they are on a gigantic scale. In other early churches we have piers of the same kind; for instance, at Eberbach; and at St. Martin, St. Maurice, the nave of St. Mary

---

* I use this expression to describe a pier very common both in England, France and Germany, consisting of a number of *shafts set in square recesses*, according to Mr. Rickman's phraseology. A plan of such a pier is given in Plate 4.

† The running tablet or cornice below the triforium.

Capitoline, and St. Aposteln at Cologne. And this occurs in many churches which seem not to have been intended for vaulting, as, for instance, Limburg on the Haardt, Schwarzach near Rastadt in part, the old church at Schaffhausen in part, the Obermünster Kirche at Ratisbon. We find, however, in such early churches, and, perhaps, as a form more prevalent in the earliest times, the arches supported by columns, of proportions nearly classical, and sometimes with a classical diminution of diameter upwards. These columns have very frequently a *cushion* capital. Such columns occur in the apses of St. Mary Capitoline, St. Peter's at Gelnhausen, in the curious old church of St. George at Cologne, in the churches at Schwarzach, Schaffhausen, and the Schotten-kirche at Ratisbon.

In other instances we find in the intermediate piers the columns *engaged* in the sides of a square pillar. In these cases they have more commonly, so far as I have observed, capitals resembling the Corinthian, and these often very well executed, as, for instance, St. Andrew at Cologne, St. Castor at Coblentz.

In such cases, the introduction of a thick roll-formed transverse vaulting-rib instead of a flat one seems to belong to a very early stage of the progress of the art. See St. Cecilia, St. Pantaleon and Ems.

When we advance from these Romanesque churches to the Early German ones, we find the intermediate piers in some respects changed. In a great number of churches the secondary pier becomes much larger and broader than before, a change which seems to be connected with the peculiarity of the triforium which we shall shortly have to mention. Thus at Sinzig,

Andernach, Boppart, Bacharach; in Notre Dame and
St. Florian at Coblentz; and at Limburg on the Lahn,
we have such low piers. At Bamberg, Gelnhausen,
and Seligenstadt, they are not so low. In the cases
where the pier arches are not in pairs, all the piers
have of course vaulting pillars, as at Bonn.

The pier arches are sometimes round and sometimes pointed, without any apparent rule as to order of
time: they retain the former figure in instances where
the pointed arch is copiously introduced in other parts,
and the style considerably developed, as, for example,
at Bonn. The round arch is found in this situation
at Bonn, and at Andernach; at Notre Dame, St. Florian, and St. John at Coblentz; at Sinzig, Andernach,
Boppart, Bacharach,—on the Rhine; and at Arnstein
on the Lahn. The pointed arch occurs at Bamberg,
Limburg, Seligenstadt, Gelnhausen, and Heimersheim.

The arch is often merely a square-edged opening
with no mouldings whatever. Sometimes it has a rebated edge, and sometimes a roll, but very seldom
any further ornament.

2. *Triforium.*

I speak next of the *Triforium;* and here I observe,
that this member does not seem to have entered into
the idea of the original Romanesque architects. The
space over the pier arches and under the clerestory
windows which the slope of the roof of the aisles occa-
sioned, is left a blank, often with a rather awkward
effect, in the finest early buildings. Thus, at Laach
and Eberbach, we have not even a moulding to occupy

it. At St. George, St. Ursula, St. Gereon (choir) and St. Maurice, the case is the same. In the three great Romanesque cathedrals we have a horizontal moulding and some pannel edges, but no important feature. This horizontal moulding occurs also at St. Andrew, where it is enriched with excellent foliage; at St. Cecelia, and in many other Romanesque buildings.

In England, in our Norman buildings, and almost constantly in the later ones, this space in large churches is filled by a row of openings or pannelings, of various kinds. It is mostly, however, a merely ornamental member, and I do not know that it was ever applied to any customary use.

But in the Early German churches the case is different. In almost all that decidedly belong to this class, we have, instead of the blank wall of the former style, a large open gallery forming a second story to the side aisle. And in most of these instances, or at least in the churches on the Rhine above Bonn, this gallery is still appropriated to a particular part of the congregation, namely, the young men, and is generally called the *Männerchor*, or as I was told at Sinzig, the *Mannhaus*. This gallery naturally makes it convenient to have the pier arches somewhat low, which it has been already observed is the case. The openings of this gallery, which of course stand immediately over the pier arches, are variously arranged. Often there is a large plain semi-circular arch, which however has frequently shafts at the sides when the pier below is plain. In Notre Dame at Coblentz, in Heimersheim and Bacharach, and in Ditkirchen on the

Lahn, this is the case, though the latter has the appearance of being a Romanesque building with these openings cut afterwards. But the more general arrangement is to have this round-headed opening subdivided into two or three subordinate openings separated by shafts which are often in pairs. This is the form which obtains at Sinzig, Boppart, Andernach and Limburg on the Lahn.

At Bamberg this Männerchor is wanting, perhaps because the usage on which it depended was local. It is remarkable that none of the churches at Cologne possess such a gallery (except St. Mary Lyskirchen, where it is not so appropriated, and is apparently later than the building.) There are in that city several instances of ornamented triforiums. St. Aposteln, which seems to stand on the boundary line between the Romanesque and Early German style, has a series of round-arched *pannels on shafts**. St. Cunibert, which is a decided example of the latter style, has a similar row of pannels. Bonn, at the border of the district occupied by the churches where the Männerchor is general, and which belongs to the same period, has a row of pointed pannels on shafts, but no gallery. St. Sebaldus at Nuremberg resembles Bonn. Limburg, in another part of the country, has an open gallery, and likewise a row of pointed pannels above. Arnstein, also situated on the Lahn, and resembling Limburg in its form, has a blank wall in the triforium.

In the construction where we have the Männerchor, there are of course two roofs to the side aisles,

---

* That is, the shafts support the arches and separate the pannels.

D

and they are generally both of the earliest or Roman kind of vaulting with no diagonal ribs. There is one remarkable exception at Sinzig, where the vaulting of the Mannhaus is of a kind, which, from its ribs, might be called tripartite, and which has two cells in the outer wall corresponding to one pier arch. As the lower vaulting of the aisle is the plain quadripartite, two windows of the Mannhaus correspond to one of the aisle, and stand in quincuncial positions to them. In other cases there are two rows of windows in the aisle which correspond to each other in a regular manner.

3. *Clerestory.*

Next, as to the *Clerestory.* The small round-headed window is almost universal in early buildings, and continues with little alteration, except perhaps an increase of size, after the vaulting and other parts have become pointed. But the disposition of these windows is often remarkable. In Romanesque buildings two small windows near one another are placed in the head of each semi-circular compartment, and thus the clerestory windows no longer answer to those below, even when the number is the same. This collocation must be considered as belonging to a very early style, inasmuch as it depends upon the supposed necessity of using a semi-circular arch. It is found in the monastery of Ebrach; in the three great cathedrals of this style (less marked, however, at Worms and Spires) and in the Romanesque churches of St. George, St. Martin and St. Cecilia. In the succeeding style, this arrangement also obtains at Andernach, though the transverse arches of the vault-

ing are there pointed. At Bacharach and Boppart we
have two rows of triforium windows, one below the
vaulting capitals and one above, but it is difficult to
say if this was the original intention.

In many Romanesque churches, however, we have
but one clerestory window in each compartment of the
vaulting; and if in this case the compartments are subdivided into two in the aisles, we have twice as many
windows below as above. This is the case in the ancient church of Laach; and this arrangement is adopted
in the succeeding style at Bamberg and Limburg.

Besides these forms of the clerestory, which are common to the Romanesque and the Transition, we have
frequently in the latter style windows of a new kind
introduced. Thus, at Bonn, we have triads of windows of which the center one is highest; but this form,
though very common in Early English, is not general
in Early German. A window which is frequently
found and peculiar to this style, is a *fan-shaped*
window, which may be described as the upper part of a
circle (more than half) of which the circumference is cut
into round notches. This obtains in the clerestory of
Sinzig, and of the dome of St. Gereon (which latter,
however, has another range of windows above). The
same window is found in the side aisles of Bonn, St.
Cunibert, St. Gereon, and Notre Dame at Coblentz.

In speaking of the vaulting shafts, their capitals
were not particularly described. In the earlier Transition buildings, the capital is often a bell-shaped block,
or some similar form, with a square abacus; at a somewhat later period of the change, we have upright leaves
like those of the Early English, still with a square aba-

cus. This square abacus must be considered as a Romanesque feature, and the Gothic is not complete where it occurs; but it is one of the last traces of the transition style which we lose. In England this form disappears at a much earlier period of the change. In the course of the transition, we have often two square abacuses set obliquely to each other in the vaulting, as at Bonn and Seligenstadt; and this occurs also in England, as at Romsey. In triple shafts, there is sometimes over the center one a projecting angle in the abacus, as at Ebrach near Bamberg.

Afterwards, we have the polygonal abacus which properly belongs to the Gothic, and under it either woven foliage, or crumpled leaves, or not unfrequently two rows of flowers, as at Oppenheim, and in several of the cathedrals of the Netherlands. The round abacus, so common in our Early English buildings, is found but rarely in Germany; it occurs in the shafts between the choir windows at Remagen and Heimersheim.

4. *Aisle Windows.*

The windows of the side aisles have been already described in speaking of clerestory windows; and the pillars of the aisle vaulting which stand between the windows have been mentioned in treating of vaulting. The wall in Romanesque and Early German churches has seldom any ornaments interiorly, and the windows have generally plain sides.

5. *Apse.*

The *apse* is generally distinguished from the rest of the building by various peculiarities of architecture.

In small churches it has mostly no aisle, to which however St. Mary Capitoline is a fine exception. The east end of Worms has also an aisle. These apses generally consist of two stories of arches on pillars, some of the arches being open as windows. The pillars are various; single, as in the transepts of St. Mary Capitoline, and most small churches; or double, as in the choir of the same church. One of the alterations which takes place in passing to the Early German style is, that these shafts come to be clustered, often in threes, often banded; sometimes, as at Remagen with a round abacus, though this is a resemblance to Early English shafts, which is rarely found in Germany. There is no part of the building where the transition from the earlier to the later style is more marked than in the apse. The form becomes polygonal instead of circular; the sides of the polygon are extended up-wards into *vaulting-escutcheons**; slender shafts, often banded, are placed in the angles of the polygon; the windows become pointed and are flanked by shafts; there are openings above the windows in the escut-cheons, and the whole structure assumes an appear-ance of being elongated upwards, and of having its parts drawn into a slender and delicate form. This description applies to the east ends of Gelnhausen, Seligenstadt, Limburg, Sinzig, Heimersheim; to St. Severin at Cologne; the north and south apses of Bonn; the west ends of Mentz, Worms, Bamberg and St. Sebaldus at Nuremberg.

---

* The wall at the ends of the pointed vaulting-cells has the form of an inverted escutcheon, and is here designated by that word.

In Heimersheim and Remagen, which are small and ill-executed churches, we have apse windows which are comparatively tall and narrow. If we suppose the same plan to be adopted on a larger and more complete scale, we shall have an easy transition to the splendid, lofty and transparent polygons which form the apses in the fully developed Gothic.

6. *Intermediate Compartment.*

The *compartment next the apse* is very often differently constructed from those which make up the remainder of the church; especially in Romanesque churches. In those which have a transept, this compartment generally fills up the *intermediate space* between the apse and the crossing of the transept; and in these cases it is very often without its windows above. This circumstance may sometimes have arisen from this part of the church having towers built against the outside. This blank occurs, for instance, at Laach, at the east end of Spires and Worms, and also at Mentz, though here this compartment has the cupola over it. Among the *transverse-triapsal** churches of Cologne, St. Martin and St. Aposteln have the upper part of the walls of this compartment filled up by two stories of small arches, some on shafts and some on little pilasters. St. Mary Capitoline has it with arches below and above like the other compartments of the apse,

---

* Viz. the churches which have apses at the ends of the transept, as well as of the choir. They are to be distinguished from *parallel-triapsal* churches, where we have three apses all towards the east. See p. 37.

but without any opening. Something similar is the case in most of the other churches of that style. Perhaps the object was to give effect to the windows of the apse, which were generally filled with fine stained glass, by admitting no lateral light to distract the eye in their immediate neighbourhood.

Features, in many respects similar, mark this part of the church in the succeeding style. At Andernach, Bonn and Boppart it is blank. At Sinzig, Limburg, and in Notre Dame at Coblentz, it has peculiar decorations in the triforium and clerestory, which, sometimes, as at Limburg, are the continuation of those in the transept. The lower story is often occupied by an arcade; and not unfrequently in the Early German churches, this consists of strong trefoil-headed arches on shafts or corbels, or intermixed. This we have at Seligenstadt, Gelnhausen, the west end of St. Sebaldus at Nuremberg, and of the cathedral at Bamberg.

The lower part of this intermediate compartment is often modified by the intention of adapting it to the stalls, with which it was to be filled up. On this account, the vaulting pillars often spring from corbels, as at Bonn and St. Severin, or from the triforium tablet, as at Bamberg.

In the last-mentioned church, the western choir is flanked by the two western doors; and to separate the choir from the aisles, which thus become entries, there are original stone screens which have trefoil-headed pannels, rich shafts, and sculpture. We have similar partitions at Mentz and at Limburg, and probably at other places, though these screens are often later.

7. *Transept.*

The decorations of the *transept* are for the most part a continuation of the members of the nave or choir. These members are however frequently somewhat modified, but it is difficult to give any general account of the alterations which occur.

The mode of constructing the *ends* is sometimes characteristic. In the early and simple Romanesque churches, it is very common to have two plain small windows below and one above, as in the ruined church of St. Peter's at Gelnhausen, in the old church of Eberbach, and in St. Castor at Coblentz. In other churches, as at Spires (and this is the case with many Norman churches) we have three or more stories, and in each story, two round-headed windows.

But in the Early German style, there is a disposition to use triads of windows, and also very commonly circular windows variously ornamented, as at Bamberg, Ebrach, Gelnhausen and Mentz; in which cases the round windows are plates perforated with openings, so as to approach to the effect of tracery. These circular windows are also found in the west ends, as in St. Paul's at Worms, and in Limburg; and on a smaller scale in the sides of the polygonal apse, as in the cathedral at Worms; or in the escutcheons of these sides, as at Gelnhausen.

V. Exterior.

I have now to mention the *parts of the exterior*, and of these, the most important are—the windows, the

mode of ornamenting the side walls, the apse, the fronts
(the west end and the transept ends,) and the use of
porches and of buttresses.

1. *Windows.*

The *windows* have little variety. They are generally, both in Romanesque and Early German work,
small and round-headed: in the latter style, however,
they are sometimes pointed and sometimes also accompanied by a roll moulding. It has already been noticed,
that as the Early German advances, the windows are
sometimes found in triads with the center one tallest.

2. *Corbel Table.*

The almost universal decoration of Romanesque
side-walls, is the corbel table with circular *notches,*
and with *pilaster strips* * between the windows running
up into it: and this is found in great profusion in
most of the examples of that, and also of the succeeding style. In some of the cases where the workmanship
is rich, as at Laach, we have flowers, &c. in the *notch
spaces* of the corbel table, and the edges of the notches
formed into a roll moulding: but to employ any other
moulding, or to make the form of the notches pointed,
as at Bamberg, belongs to the later style. This corbel
table is replaced, in the transept end of Bamberg,
and the neighbouring church of Ebrach, by a peculiar
ornament with semi-circular horizontal notches.

---

* I use the term *pilaster-strips* to designate projections from the
wall, which are about the breadth and proportion of pilasters, but
have no capitals, and pass into the corbel table.

3. *Apse.*

In very plain churches the Romanesque corbel table also runs round the head of the *apse* wall. But in the greater number of the churches of that style the apse is finished in a manner very peculiar. The windows are placed in round-headed pannels which are on shafts or pilasters, and run in one or two stories. Over these is an *apsidal gallery and cornice:* the gallery consists of open round-headed arches standing on small shafts two or three feet high, and *set two deep* * : and in this line of shafts, groups of four, or other distinctions, occur at regular intervals. Above this, is a bold projecting moulding, consisting generally of two quarter-rounds with a hollow between, the lower round being cut into billets, the upper one enriched with leaves as classical mouldings often are. Below the gallery is in most cases a line of small rectangular sunk pannels. This particular combination of ornaments is employed with remarkable consistency and uniformity in a great number of Romanesque churches, as St. Mary Capitoline, St. Martin, St. Castor at Coblentz, the east end of Mentz, Spires, &c.: Laach is an exception.

And this mode of ornamenting the apse is employed with equal constancy in the next style, as for instance in the west end of the cathedrals of Worms and Mentz:

---

* Shafts set two deep are a very common mode of enriching Romanesque buildings, and date apparently from a very early period. They are found for instance in the cloisters adjacent to the ancient churches of Laach, Zurich, and Aschaffenburg. They exist also in many ancient buildings in Italy, and in the palace of Frederic Barbarossa at Gelnhausen.

in the east ends of St. Paul's at Worms, Andernach, Bacharach, Sinzig, Bonn and Bamberg.

At Limburg the gallery has square-headed, at Geln-hausen trefoil-headed openings.

These open galleries certainly give great richness and beauty to the upper parts of the buildings where they are used, and seem to have been favourite deco-rations with the architects. They are often carried along other parts of the building besides the apse. Thus at Spires they are continued all round: at St. Aposteln they run along the square part of the east end: and the octagons which occur in Romanesque and Early German buildings are often thus enriched; as at Worms, (both octagons), at St. Aposteln and St. Ge-reon.

It is also to be noted with regard to the apses of the Early German churches, that we see in them the butt-ress beginning to appear, though very flat and small. It has generally a triangular or *gable* head. See Mentz, the west end, and Bamberg, the west end.

In later work the galleries are carried along the clerestory, with arches somewhat larger, and often pointed, as at Limburg and Bonn.

4. *Towers.*

The Romanesque *towers* and those which succeeded them have at first sight a great resemblance; both con-sist of a number of stories with corbel tables and round-headed pannelings and openings to most of the stories. The trefoil-headed pannel as well as the round-headed one appears to occur in very early work, as for in-stance at St. Castor and Laach.

On a closer examination however it seems not impossible to find differences between the towers of the two styles. The square towers have often their sides terminated upwards by a gable, so as to make the covering a square pyramid set on diagonal-wise upon the square of the tower. In the earlier churches these gables or pediments have not acute angles, and they are bounded both at the lower edge and at the inclined edges by a strongly marked cornice. The towers of the Early German style have, at least often, a more acute pediment, with the cornices, especially the horizontal one, more slight, as for instance the west tower of St. Aposteln.

The four towers of Bamberg, which must be considered as belonging to the transition style, are of a very rich and peculiar character, and, like the rest of that noble cathedral, of very excellent work.

Other differences are to be found in the corbel tables of the later churches. At Andernach, Boppart, Limburg, &c. besides the usual corbel table, there are, over the windows, in several of the tower stories, lines having embattled or wavy forms, and variously enriched. When the openings become pointed, the shafts banded, or clustered, or much multiplied, and the mouldings deeper and more complex, the features of the newer style are more obvious, as at Bonn, Sinzig, Heimersheim and Gelnhausen.

5. *Fronts.*

The *fronts*, and the west fronts in particular, of Romanesque and Early German churches, are not commonly distinguished by any very remarkable features.

In many instances of the former style, as has been observed, the west end is an apse as well as the east. Laach, where this is the case, has a square court with cloisters, which forms a sort of portal to the church: so also has St. Mary Capitoline. At Lorsch the very old and curious chapel which is still preserved seems to have been a part of such a portal space *.

In most early buildings, where there is a west front, it has a few round-headed openings at the ends of the side-aisles, as at Eberbach.

But there are few cases where these fronts are visible as constructed by the Romanesque architects. They are often concealed by their connection with other buildings, or superseded by later erections.

In the west fronts of the succeeding style, and also in the transept ends, we have often to remark doors with pointed arches, detached and banded shafts, and enriched roll mouldings, which to an eye accustomed to English architecture have a more completely Gothic character than the other parts. This may be noticed at St. Gereon, St. Cunibert, Sinzig, Andernach, Bonn and Limburg.

A mode of ornamenting the roll mouldings of the arch, which is very common in these cases, is to give it bands, as if it were a shaft, at certain intervals: for instance, at the highest point, and at the middle points of the two sides of the arch. Another ornament which is common, is a little roll or *rouleau* placed transversely under the summit of the arch, so that its circular end just occupies the arch-point.

---

* We find similar portal cloisters in Italy, as in the church of St. Ambrose at Milan.

The arrangement of windows in the transept end has been mentioned in speaking of the interior. Exteriorly the transept has often a pilaster or *buttress-strip** dividing the front into two halves, with windows on each side. This arrangement is also that of our Norman buildings. At Spires the pilasters have good Corinthian capitals, and the architraves of the windows are enriched.

Here may be mentioned the fronts of the old cathedrals which are found in the north of Germany, as at Brunswick and Goslar. They consist of a wall of very plain work pierced with a window flanked by octagonal towers, which have round-headed openings subdivided into double openings by shafts.

The Italian Romanesque fronts have generally one or more circular windows. and a quantity of arcades, horizontal and sloping, with other enrichments, and also the curious portico shortly to be described.

6. *Porches.*

We here speak of *Porches,* so far as they are to be found in these styles of architecture. In our Norman buildings in England such a member sometimes appears; but a distinct porch is not found in the Romanesque churches of Germany. In Italy, at least in Lombardy, it appears to be a common part of the earliest buildings. Several of the old and curious churches of Verona, as St. Zeno and the cathedral, have a remarkable portico, and this, from the representation in Mr. Kerrich's paper in Vol. xvi. of the Archæologia, appears to occur also at Placentia, Modena and Parma.

---

* A broad flat buttress of slight projection.

This portico consists of a covering projecting from the wall of the church, and supported at each side by one or more pillars. The covering has a triangular pediment and sloping roof above, and a barrel vault below: and is very often in two stories, as in the cathedral at Verona, Placentia, Modena and Parma; and sometimes in one story only, as at St. Zeno. The pillars at the sides generally rest on lions or other animals, and when there are more than one pair, as at Verona, are varied in their proportions and capitals, and are some of them twisted, &c. A portico similar to those of one story occurs on the south side of the cathedral of Trent; one somewhat different, with groining, being found on the north side of the same church.

In the German churches the style which succeeded the Romanesque has often porches at the west end of the church, consisting of a few compartments of groining (generally two) supported by pillars. Such porches are found at St. Martin, St. Cunibert and St. Gereon.

Another member having some analogy to a porch should be noticed. It consists in the front of a porch stuck against the wall; that is, the door, instead of being in the plain wall, is opened in a compartment having a slight projection, and bounded by upright returns to the right and left of the door. This *projecting face* of wall is sometimes ornamented with sculpture, of which the Schotten-kirche at Ratisbon is a very curious example. At other times it has only the mouldings of the other part of the wall, occasionally with the addition of the foliage of the capitals of the door-shafts continued as a running moulding. Instances are Andernach, Bamberg and St. Sebaldus at Nuremberg.

This is found, so far as I have observed, principally in Early German work.

The doors in most of these cases are round-headed, and have the tympanum filled up and enriched with sculpture. And in such doors, the lintel which bounds the tympanum below has its upper edge formed into a low pediment.

7. *Buttresses.*

It must be considered remarkable that in the Romanesque style, where the vaulting is often very large and bold, *buttresses* seem to have been unknown, their place being supplied by the enormous thickness of the walls, and by the lowness of the spring of the arch, which threw much of the thrust of the main-aisle vaulting upon the vaults of the side aisles. Perhaps the hollowing out segmental spaces in the wall between the pillars (as in St. Castor at Coblentz) may be considered as an artifice indicating a perception of the possibility of employing buttresses instead of a uniformly thick wall; and when we arrive at the Early German style, we find buttresses make their appearance, as in the west end and transept of Mentz, at Seligenstadt, Heimersheim, Sinzig, &c. They are however in all these cases of small projection; are terminated usually with a plain triangular capping, and are not otherwise made conspicuous. It is not till we come to the next style, (the complete or *Decorated* Gothic) that the advantage of them seems to have been fully perceived. In that style buttresses of deep projection, and often flying-buttresses, are used in a profuse and almost wanton manner to elevate into the air clerestories of vast height and of the most open and diaphanous workmanship, and thus they are the main instruments in giving to the structures of that period the extraordinary elevation and lightness by which they are characterized.

It will I think appear from the account which has been given of the transition style of Germany, that the introduction of the *pointed arch* was by no means immediately accompanied by all the other changes which distinguish the Gothic from the Romanesque. The old forms and tendencies lingered long, and were replaced gradually. And the Early German architecture for a considerable period offers an image of the conflict and indecision of a revolution which is to end in replacing the prevailing principles by their opposites. At last the new character struggled fairly through and freed itself from the fragments of the older system. And if we would select the most important of the improvements by which this complete developement was effected, we must, I conceive, fix upon the introduction of the *flying-buttress*. The inventor of this exemplification of architectural and mechanical skill must be considered as having done, for the advancement of Gothic architecture, far more than the inventor of the pointed arch: or rather as having given the means of executing in their full extent, those wonderful works of which the pointed arch contained the first imperfect rudiment and suggestion.

It would hardly be too fanciful to consider the newer religious architecture as bearing the impress of its Christian birth, and exhibiting in the leading lines of its members, and the aspiring summits of its edifices,

E

forms " whose silent finger points to heaven." And
this idea becomes more striking still when we compare
our religious buildings with the graceful but low and
level outline of the temples of heathen antiquity, whose
favorite purpose seems to be to spread along and beau-
tify the earth which their worshippers deified. We
may thus, with the poet's as well as the artist's pleasure, image to ourselves

> ———— the bulk
> Of ancient Minster lifted above the cloud
> Of the dense air which town or city breeds
> To intercept the sun's glad beams ;

and leaving far below it the pillared front and long
entablature of the Grecian portico : while the *buttressed*
clerestory, with its spiry pinnacles and woven tracery,
hangs over the altar and the sanctuary, like a coronal
upheld by the stony arms which the Christian architects
learnt to make powerful and obedient for this purpose.

SECT. 3. *On the Complete Gothic Style in Germany.*

The progress of the style of which the characters
have now been indicated led to the formation of the
Complete Gothic. This style I shall not dwell upon ;
it is almost sufficient to refer to Mr. Rickman's account of the Decorated English, and to the English
specimens which exemplify that kind of architecture.
The resemblance obtains not only in the general forms
of the members and parts, but in the details also, the
canopies, bases, profiles of mouldings, &c.

The earliest form of the Complete Gothic in Germany has, throughout, *geometrical tracery.* Cologne
cathedral is the unrivalled glory of buildings of this

class; the most splendid, and perhaps the earliest exhibition of the beauties of this style. The abbey of Altenberg, at a little distance from Cologne, now a manufactory, had a church of the same admirable style, which still exists. This is said to have been built by the same person who was the architect of Cologne; and as it was finished, we are enabled, from the exquisite lightness and grace of its lofty interior, to form some conception of the splendid and majestic vision which would have been embodied by the completion of the original plan of Cologne. The church of Altenberg is particularly worthy of notice for the beautiful and varied forms of its window tracery, which in the interior view are seen to singular advantage, the glass being ornamented in white and grey patterns, which subdue without colouring the light*. The church of St. Catharine at Oppenheim, near Worms, also in part a ruin, is another fine example of this style, and has been worthily illustrated in the magnificent work of Mr. Müller. These buildings are remarkable for a purity and simplicity in their details which our Decorated Style does not always possess.

The splendid cathedral of Strasburg belongs to the same class as that at Cologne, and has some of the same peculiarities. Among other examples of prodigality of ornament, we have in both these buildings *double planes of tracery*; that is, two tracery windows or frames one

---

* It is melancholy to see this beautiful building tending to decay: perhaps a short time will deprive it of the advantage which its present completeness gives it over its more magnificent sister of Cologne. The roof is insufficient, and the south transept is broken down, so that the church seems marked out as a prey to speedy ruin.

behind another in the same opening; the pattern of the tracery being often different in the two. This extravagance (for it almost deserves to be so called) appears in the towers at Cologne; at Strasburg it is carried to such an extent in the west front, that the building looks as if it were placed behind a rich open screen, or in a cage of woven stone. The effect of this construction is certainly very gorgeous, but with a sacrifice of distinctness from the multiplicity and intersections of the lines. Freyburg is another great church with obvious resemblances to Strasburg; it is a very fine building, but is remarkable rather for the beauty of its composition and form, than for the delicacy of its details; nothing, however, can be more admirable than the open work of its matchless spire.

At a period a little later, we have *flowing tracery*, and this occurs with most abundant variety of form in most of the Gothic buildings: among others, in the cathedral at Freyburg, and with some very curious features in that at Strasburg.

Other buildings belonging to the complete Gothic style, are St. Thomas and St. Lefrau at Oberwesel; St. Werner, in ruins, at Bacharach; Lorch on the opposite side of the Rhine; St. Stephen, St. Quintin and St. Christopher at Mentz; a very beautiful church and a chapel at Kidrich near Elfeld; the cathedral at Frankfort; the church at Neustadt on the Haardt; the cathedral at Ratisbon, and the church of the Minorites, now the Halle, in that city; St. Sebaldus, St. Lawrence, &c. at Nuremburg; St. Mary and the Deutsche Haus at Wurzburg; and many others in almost every city in Germany.

Several of these buildings probably belong to different ages; for the separation of the pure Gothic from the styles into which it degenerated requires a particular study, and a scrupulous discrimination which it has not been my purpose at present to exercise.

CHAP. III.

SECT. 1. *On describing Churches.*

By comparing actual buildings with descriptions conveyed in precise and determinate phraseology, such as is that of Mr. Rickman, the architectural observer will become aware how completely words alone may avail to preserve and transmit distinct and adequate conceptions of an edifice. And when he has thus begun to feel the import and value of a technical language, a little practice and contrivance will enable him thus to register for himself, or for others, the principal features of any building which may attract his notice. If he should happen to visit the churches of Germany, it is hoped that the classifications and terms introduced in the preceding pages may be of service in enabling him to discover and characterize the most remarkable of their peculiarities. And should he examine the churches referred to in the previous Chapters, or other similar buildings not familiar to the English reader, of which there exist in Germany a great number possessing very interesting characters, he may, by recording their peculiarities, contribute to throw light upon the history of architecture; for in this study, as in all others, any sound speculation must be founded on the accurate knowledge of an extensive collection of particular instances. If for this, or for any other purpose, he should make his memoranda concerning a number of churches in succession, some *method* in doing this may be of service. The subdivisions employed in the preceding descriptions indicate the points to which the attention is to be directed; and these may be made a guide in the survey of each church. But besides this general enumeration, several rules of order and selection will probably occur to the observer, tending to facilitate and expedite his labour; and such as have occurred to one person, may possibly be of some use to others. Under this impression, the following directions are offered to the reader, being such as I found it in general convenient to follow, in the course of the observations which gave rise to the preceding pages.

In describing a church, mention first what is the GENERAL STYLE of the work (Romanesque, Transition, Complete Gothic, Perpendicular, &c.) for this both conveys a general notion of its appearance, and modifies the interpretation of the terms afterwards used.

Describe next the GROUND-PLAN, and then the VAULTING: for these being given, the number and position of almost all the members is determined, and the rest of the description will have a reference to a known arrangement of parts. In the vaulting, mention whether it is Roman vaulting, or some other form of quadripartite, or sexpartite, &c. ; if quadripartite, whether both transverse and longitudinal ribs are pointed ; whether in single or double compartments; the ribs where they occur, their form and mouldings; and whether the side aisles are of the same kind as the center aisle.

Describe next one COMPARTMENT of the inside, selecting that which is most frequently repeated: and noticing—first the *piers*, whether they are columns, pilasters, shafts and pier-edges, clustered shafts, or piers of clustered mouldings, and what the difference is of the *intermediate* piers if any: their *capitals*, whether Corinthian, cushion, sculpture, upright leaves, woven foliage, &c.: the *aisles*, whether they have pillars like those of the piers, (their vaulting having been already noticed,) what are the windows, and whether the wall is ornamented;—then the *pier-arches*, whether round or pointed, and whether the arch is plain, rebated, chamfered, or with what mouldings:—then the *triforium;* whether blank, pannelled, of detached shafts with wall behind, or of openings; the openings whether single, or double, &c.; or subdivided; and if either double or subdivided, how separated, whether by shafts, clustered shafts, pilasters, &c.; and whether with round or pointed openings:—then the *clerestory;* the windows, whether single, in pairs, or in triads; if not single, how separated; with what mouldings; what capitals to the vaulting shafts: and throughout, what capitals there are to shafts, and what mouldings are used, when they offer any thing remarkable.

Afterwards, notice any peculiarities or deviations from this compartment which appear in the *apse*, the *intermediate compartment*, the *transepts;* in the supporting piers of the *crossing;* and at the *west end.*

In describing the EXTERIOR, the order of description does not appear to be of much consequence. The most important points are, the number and position of the *towers*, whether they are at the east, at the crossing, &c.;

whether their sides end in gables, and whether these
have strong or light cornices, especially the horizontal
lines; how the different stories of the towers are decorated : — the *apses*, whether round or polygonal;
whether they have the peculiar *apsidal gallery* of the
Romanesque : — the finishing of the wall; whether by
a corbel table with notches, round or pointed, plain
or moulded; or by a cornice, balustrade, canopies,
pinnacles, &c. The *buttresses* also, or their absence,
should be remarked : what projection they have, what
offsets, what termination, how ornamented. *Flying
buttresses* are to be noticed, and how they are stopped
and supported at the lower end. Finally, the *west
front* is a leading part of the building when it is ornamented, and the *porches* in the other parts; and these
portions often contain the richest and most ornamented
workmanship in the whole edifice. If the church has
many subordinate members externally, and is remarkable in detail, it may be proper to take notes of a
single *compartment* externally, from the ground to the
roof in order. The *windows* in particular will require
attention; the mouldings of the window-sides, the dripstones, canopies and pannellings which accompany them :
and especially the *tracery*. If any one were to observe,
in succession, a great number of different windows of
the complete Gothic, he would probably be led to de-
vise some simple and technical phraseology or notation
by which the form of the tracery might be conveyed;
but this does not fall within the main purpose of the
present Essay.

Sect. 2. *Nomenclature.*

The clearness and definiteness of an architectural description must depend upon the use of terms accurately defined and steadily employed. The phraseology introduced by Mr. Rickman should be made the basis of such a language; but in applying this to foreign architecture, which he had not in view, it becomes convenient to introduce several additional words and phrases. Some of these have been made use of in the preceding pages, and they ave generally been explained when first employed. The following is a list of such words, with a few others which we have also had occasion to illustrate.

List of Technical Terms which are explained in the preceding pages.

SECT. 3. *On a Notation to express Vaulting.*

Though the different forms of vaults may be described with sufficient distinctness by means of the terms already explained, viz. by referring them to their class as quadripartite, sexpartite, &c. and by noticing whether the cells are deep or shallow, what ribs exist, whether these are pointed or round, and of what mouldings composed; yet it is often possible to represent the vaulting more immediately and distinctly to the eye by means of a few lines drawn to indicate it. Having found the convenience and simplification which arise from such a notation, I shall here give an account of the method which I have employed.

A rude plan is drawn of one compartment of the vaulting in single lines : that is, a rectangle to represent the space occupied by the compartment, and diagonal or other lines for the ribs and intersections of vaults which occur.

The straight lines which here represent *arches*, have a small cross (×) marked on their middle if the arch is *pointed :* if it be round they have no mark.

The *cells* have a mark to represent whether they are pointed or round, the mark being a small apex (∧) turned towards the intersection of the vaults if they are pointed ; and a small arc (⌒) similarly situated if they are round.

The lines which represent the principal ribs are drawn double, triple, &c. according to the magnitude and number of the mouldings : the smaller ribs being represented by a smaller number of lines, and an intersection without ribs by a single line.

Thus in Plate I, under Figures 1, 2, 3, 4, 5, 7, 8, we have the symbols by which they would on this system be represented.

A dome would in this method be represented by a circle surrounding the vertex of the dome ; and a portion of a dome by an arc of such a circle.

In the ground plan of Mentz, Fig. 9, of St. Aposteln, Fig. 10, and of Laach, Fig. 11. the vaulting is represented upon this system. The second of these churches has had, within a short time, a vaulted cieling of lath and plaster substituted for the ancient tuf vaulting. The modern form is represented by the dotted lines.

Sect. 4. *On making Architectural Notes by means of Drawing.*

It may often happen that a very rude and imperfect sketch, such as it requires little skill to produce, will represent the form and relations of some members of architecture better and more briefly than a description in words. Where a building is thus noted, the following suggestions may be useful.

Draw a single interior compartment; either as a geometrical elevation; or, what is generally better, but more difficult, as an oblique perspective view. By this means we obtain both the forms and positions of the piers, pier arches, triforium, clerestory, and vaulting. It is sufficient to represent shafts by a single or double line, with a short tranverse line for the abacus, and similar compendious representations may be employed for other parts.

If it be desirable to go into greater detail, as in good or remarkable churches it generally is, some of the following additional sketches should be added: the plan of the pier: its capital: the profile of the arch mouldings; any drawing which may be requisite to explain the combinations of shafts in the triforium and clerestory: the capitals of such shafts: the clerestory window-sides: the ornaments of the side walls: the tracery of the windows: the ends of the transept: the apse.

Externally, a general perspective view gives the grouping of the towers and their parts: the western front and the apse may also be characteristic: but such drawings are generally much more laborious and difficult than the memoranda of the interior above re-commended.

In Plate IV. Fig. 12. is represented a compart-ment of Sinzig near Bonn, which exhibits a fan-shaped window in the clerestory.

SECT. 5. *List of Churches.*

The following are the principal German churches which I examined and noted according to the method just explained. The observations made on these, com-bined with what I had before noticed, have given rise to the preceding attempt to connect and discriminate these churches. In the list, R is added to indicate that a church is principally Romanesque, G that it is of the Gothic, and T that it is of the Transition Style. The most remarkable of the churches are distinguished by an asterisk. They are arranged according to their topographical succession, first ascending the Rhine, and then diverging into Bavaria and Franconia.

Near the Rhine.

COLOGNE.
* St. Mary Capitoline.   R.
* St. Martin.   R.
  St. George.   R.
  St. Andrew.   R.   Choir. G.
* St. Gereon.   R.   Polygon. T.
* St. Aposteln.   R.
  St. Pantaleon.   R.
  St. Cecilia.   R.
* St. Cunibert.   T.
  St. Ursula.   R.   Roof. G.
  St. Mary Lyskirchen.   T.
  St. Severin.   T.
  St. Peter.   G.
* Cathedral.   G.

BONN.
  * Cathedral.   T.
  Apollinarisberg.   R.
  Remagen.   T.
  Hemersheim.   T. } on the
* Ahrweiler.   G.   } Ahr.
* Sinzig.   T.
* Andernach.   T.
* Laach.   R.
  COBLENTZ.
   * St. Castor.   R.
     Notre Dame.   T.
     St. Florian.   R.
     St. John.   T.
  Neiderlahnstein.
* Boppart.   T.

Oberwesel.
St. Lefrau. G.
St. Thomas. G.
Bacharach.
* Lutheran Church. T.
* St. Werner. G.
Lorch. G.
* Clemenskirche. R.

MENTZ.
* Cathedral. East end R.
West T.
St. Stephen. G.
St. Quintin. G.
St. Christopher. G.

RHEINGAU.
Winkel. G.
Johannisberg. R.
Eberbach near Elfeld.
* Large Abbey Church. R.
* Small do. or Hall? T.
* Cellars do. R.
Kidrich near Elfeld
* Church. G.
* St. Michael's Chapel. G.
Elfeld. G.

FRANKFORT.
Cathedral. G.
St. Leonhard. G. Apse. T.
* Oppenheim. G.
Lorsch. R.

WORMS.
* Cathedral. East end, R.
West, T.
* St. Paul. R. and T.
* St. Martin. R.
Limburg on the Haardt.
Abbey Church. R.
Neustadt. G.

SPIRES.
* Cathedral. R.
Schwarzach. R.

STRASBURG.
* Cathedral. G.
St. Stephen. R.
St. Thomas. T.
FREYBURG.
* Cathedral.
In Bavaria.
Morsburg.
LANDSHUT.
St. Eudoch. G.
St. Martin. G.
Holy Ghost. G.
RATISBON.
* Schottenkirche. R.
St. Emmeran. R.
Obermünster. R. Porch, T.
Niedermünster. R
Minorites. G.
* Cathedral. G.
Old Cathedral. R.
NUREMBERG.
St. Laurence. G.
* St. Ottmar's Chapel. R.
* St. Margaret's ―― R.
* St. Eucharius' ―― T.
* St. Sebaldus. G. West end, T.
BAMBERG.
* Cathedral. T.
Oberpfarrkirche. G.
St. Stephen, a tower. R.
Ebrach.
* Large Abbey Church. T.
(Inside modernized).
Small do. T.
WURZBURG.
St. Burckhard. R.
Schottenkirche. R.
Deutsche Haus. G.
Domkirche. R. Inside
modernized.
Neumünster. R. Inside ditto.
St. Mary. G.

On the Lahn.

LIMBURG.
 * Cathedral. T.
   Bishop's Chapel. G.
Ditkirchen. R.
Arnstein. T.
Ems. R.

In Switzerland.

Schaffhausen (old Church). R.
Zurich. R.
Lucerne. R.
Bern. G.

Plate I.

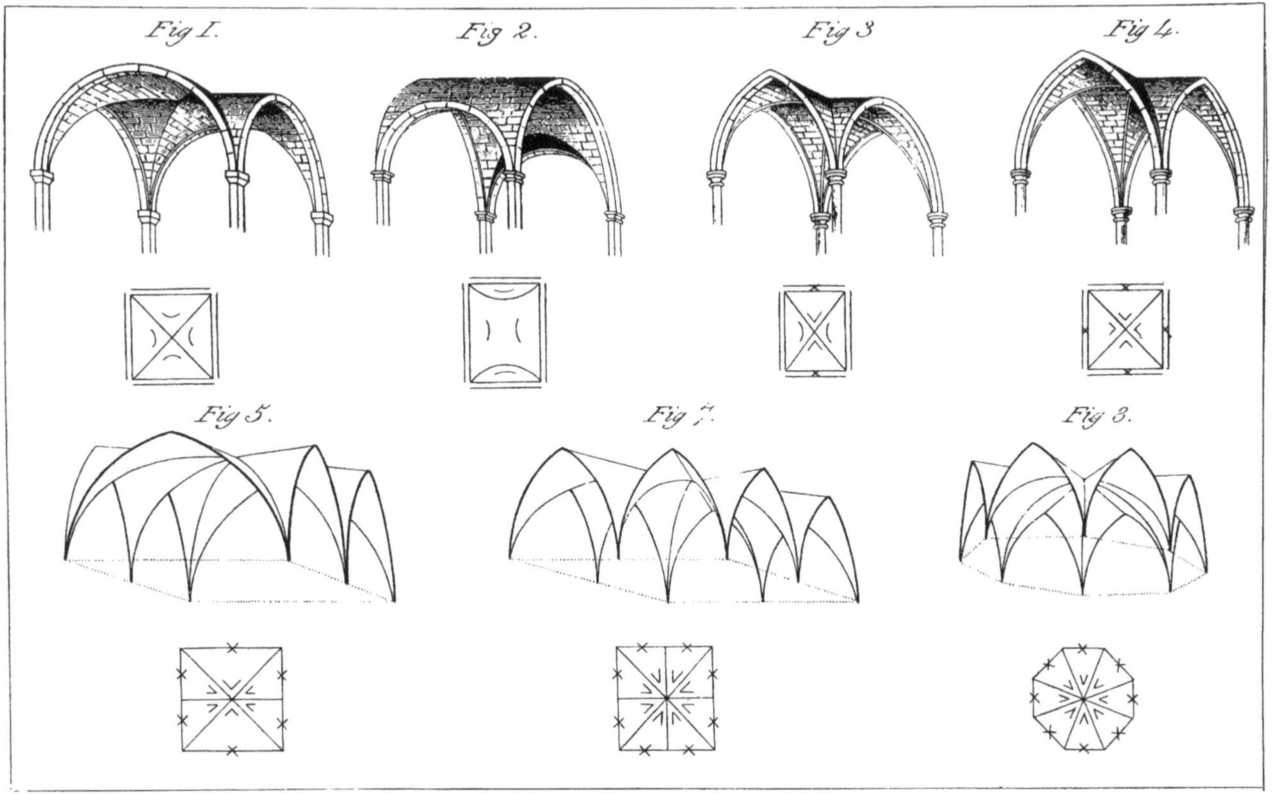

Fig 1.   Fig 2.   Fig 3   Fig 4.

Fig 5.   Fig 7.   Fig 8.

J. & H. S. Storer sc. Cambridge.

Plate II.

Fig 9. Mentz.

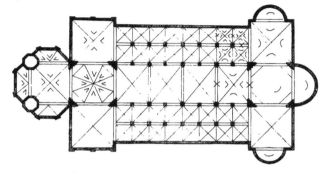

Fig. 10. St Aposteln.

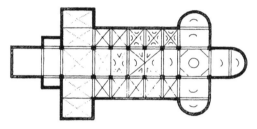

Fig. II. Laach.

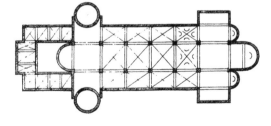

Plate IV.

Fig. 15.

Fig. 14.

Fig. 13.

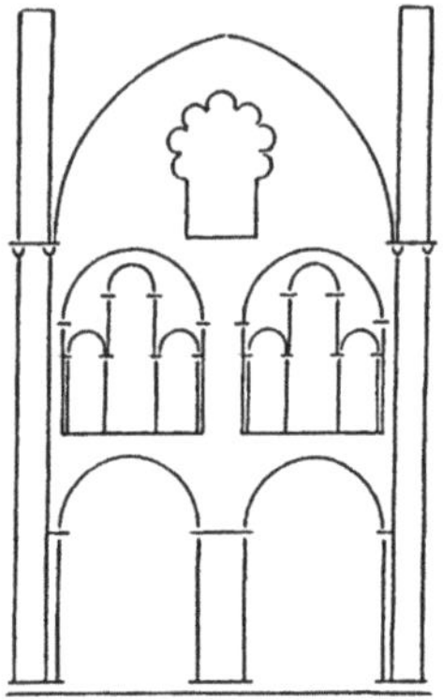

Fig. 12. Sin. zig.

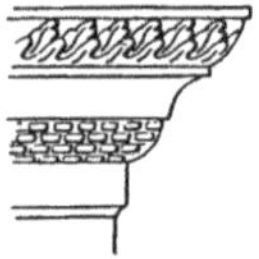

Fig. 6.

J. & J. S. Sieber sc. Cambridge.

For EU product safety concerns, contact us at Calle de José Abascal, 56–1°,
28003 Madrid, Spain or eugpsr@cambridge.org.

 www.ingramcontent.com/pod-product-compliance
Ingram Content Group UK Ltd.
Pitfield, Milton Keynes, MK11 3LW, UK
UKHW012338130625
459647UK00009B/365